Relational Da

Design and Use

Third Edition

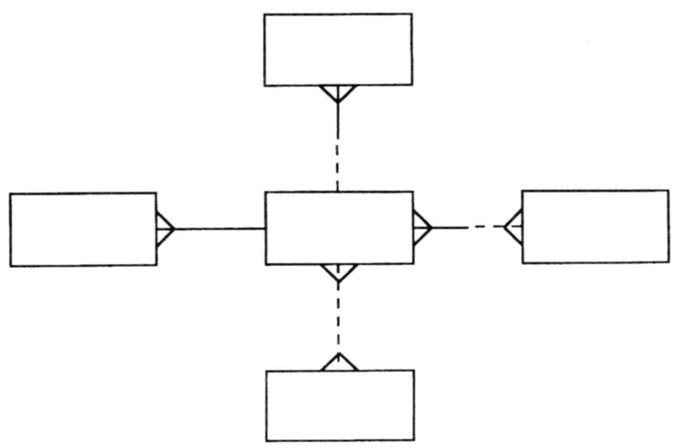

Ray Dawson

GROUP D PUBLICATIONS

Published by Group D Publications Ltd.
Loughborough, United Kingdom.

First edition published October 1997.
Second edition published April 1999,
reprinted October 2000.
Third edition published October 2001.

Printed and bound in the United Kingdom by
Audio Visual Services, Loughborough University

British Library Cataloguing-in-Publication data

A catalogue record for this book is available from the British Library

ISBN 1-874152-09-8

Copies of this book should be ordered from the author:

Ray Dawson
Department of Computer Science,
Loughborough University,
Loughborough, Leicestershire LE11 3TU

Fax: 01509-211586
Email: R.J.Dawson@Lboro.ac.UK

Contents

Software

Oracle® is a product of the Oracle® Corporation. References to Oracle throughout this book refer to Version 7 of the Oracle® database.

Access is a product of the Microsoft® Corporation. References to Access throughout this book refer to Access 97 for Windows® 95 or Windows® 97.

Visual Basic is a product of the Microsoft® Corporation. References to Visual Basic throughout this book refer to Version 5.0 of Visual Basic for Windows® 95 or Windows® 97.

Acknowledgements

I would like to thank Group D Publications for publishing this book. My thanks also go to the Department of Computer Science for providing the money and resources to enable this book to be published.

Dedication

I would like thank my wife, Dawn, and my sons, Matthew and Alex, for their support while I was producing this book. I dedicate this book to them.

Ray Dawson

CHAPTER 1

Overview

Contents | Page

1.1 Why a Book on Relational Databases?

This book is based on the experience of many years that expertise in building and handling databases is not as widespread as it should be.

Student project work often illustrates the problem. So many students eagerly start to build a database application based on what they thought was a fairly obvious data structure....

.... only to find to their cost later that the database design is causing serious difficulties.

They are then faced with the unfortunate choice of:

1. struggling on with more and more fudges to get round the inadequate data structure design,

or 2. redesigning their data structure from scratch and in the process scrapping much of the work they had done so far.

This stresses the need to get the data structure right from the start of a project....

.... this takes time and a fair degree of skill.

It is the skill aspect that seems to be so often missing and this is what this book hopes to redress.

This book is aimed to support a course on databases. It does not contain large numbers of exercises, however, as it is expected that course leaders will provide students with these themselves.

1.2 Contents Overview

This book starts with the main diagrammatic means of analysing data structure requirements - entity relationship modelling. This is a proven method of deriving a database structure for any given problem. It is not perfect but it is undoubtedly the best diagrammatic database design system on offer.

The advantage of a diagrammatic system is that it aids the thinking process. Most people think better in pictures as they need to "visualise" their work.

It is also a good communication tool. "A picture is worth a thousand words" is a saying with some meaning. It is far easier for other people to understand your reasoning if you can show your thinking in diagrammatic form.

Chapters 2 to 5 take the reader through the entity relationship modelling method of deriving a database structure and this is then illustrated in a case study in chapter 6.

Chapters 7 and 8 examine the process of database normalisation to derive a data structure. This is treated in a very "common sense" manner rather than the more mathematical approach in some texts.

Normalisation is a complex process but represents the ultimate check that a data structure is correct. It is hoped this book's approach won't be too difficult for even the most un-mathematically minded reader.

Chapter 9 attempts to further the reader's understanding by showing how entity relationship modelling and normalisation are not two completely different processes but are, in fact, closely related.

Chapter 10 then takes the reader through a case study example based on normalisation to consolidate the readers understanding of the process.

The next chapters are all concerned with SQL, the standard query language used by all major database systems on the market.

The ability to handle SQL is a skill in its own right and one which is needed by the vast majority of professional computer users.

Which is the most frequent computer language used today? C, C++, Visual Basic, Java and even Cobol are usually given as the answer this question. Yet SQL is undoubtedly used by more software professionals than any of these.

Many database systems attempt to hide the SQL from the users. It is possible to develop simple applications in Access, for example, without knowing any SQL. However, any significant development usually sees the developer manipulating the SQL directly sooner or later.

The SQL is introduced in chapter 11, with chapters 12, 13 and 15 devoted to the most complicated command, the `SELECT` statement.

Chapter 14 gives details of the SQL commands for maintaining and manipulating the data tables.

Chapter 16 describes the view, a feature available in SQL and many other database languages. The reasons for using a view are discussed as well as the syntax for creating and deleting views.

Chapter 17 looks at the performance of database management systems. The facilities provided by the software and the general methods for optimising the systems performance are described.

Chapters 18 to 21 all look at the methods for preserving database integrity.

Chapter 18 looks at the general facilities available to prevent data errors and chapter 19 looks at the particular case of referential integrity - a problem of particular importance in relational database systems.

Chapter 20 looks at features in the user interface that can assist in preventing data error, and chapter 21 looks at the particular problem of more than one user using the system at the same time.

Finally chapter 22 examines the whole software development process in relation to database systems. Prototyping is shown to be of particular relevance as it can assist in the design of the data structure, and is advocated as the main method of database system development.

1.3 Book Style

This book is written in a style which involves keeping paragraphs short, frequent itemising in point form, and separate topics on each page.

The style is perhaps more consistent with a set of notes than a text book. This is, in fact, where its origins lie. It is based on notes for modules taught to university students and on notes for short courses given to industry.

No attempt has been made to significantly change the style, however, as it not meant to be a "good read" that you would want to curl up with late at night.

This book is intended to be a working text. It will have the dual purpose of a teaching manual and a reference manual usable by both beginners and practitioners of the subject.

It is hoped the format will make the book easy to read, easy to find what the reader is looking for, and above all, easy to understand.

The reader is warned, however, understanding relational databases is not a simple matter .... you need to allow a bit of time and patience to get to the bottom of the subject!

Any constructive comments on the book can be addressed to the author directly via email on:

R.J.Dawson@Lboro.ac.UK

CHAPTER 2

Creating the Entity Relationship Diagram

Contents Page

2.1 Entity Relationship Modelling

The Objectives:

1. To help develop an understanding of the nature of the data complexities in the system.

2. To be able to organise the data into a logical, "structured" form with each data item where it may be expected (useful for maintenance).

3. To be able to organise the data in an efficient way so that data is neither duplicated nor omitted.

The End Result:

The end result is the "system data dictionary" which defines:

1. The data tables that appear in the system.

2. The fields (ie. columns) for each entry in the table.

3. A key for each table, consisting of one or more of these fields.

2.2 Step 1 - Identify the Entities and Attributes

An "**entity**" is something that has an independent existence.

Eg. *Items, Components, Sales reps, Customers*

Anything that provides information about an entity is referred to as an "**attribute**" of the entity.

Eg. *Description, Quantity, Name, Identity Number*

It may not be clear whether an item is an entity or an attribute . . . it is possible for the same thing to be an entity in one analysis, but an attribute in another.

Eg. *Shape, Tax, Manufacturer, Job*

If in doubt, make it an entity to start with.

(The analysis will later determine whether it should be an attribute)

Step 1 is a first shot at determining the data bases for a given problem, giving:

- A data table for each type of entity.
- An entry for each entity of that type.
- Fields for each data table entry to represent the attributes.

2.3 Data Tables For Entities

Eg. The employee entity for a company may have the attributes: Name, ID number, Job title, Salary.

The resulting employee table would be:

Name	ID number	Job title	Salary
Fred Bloggs	10001	Director	30,000
Joe Brown	12941	Salesman	20,000
Alice Cooke	18802	Manager	23,000
John Smith	10457	Engineer	18,000
Sarah King	13098	Accountant	28.000

A company car entity with attributes: registration number, make, model and year would give the table:

Reg.No.	Make	Model	Year
N100 ARK	Ford	Mondeo	1995
P346 VRY	Vauxhall	Astra	1996
R882 PRG	Peugeot	406	1997
N241 WET	Ford	Mondeo	1995
K318 BAR	Vauxhall	Cavalier	1992

Note: Even though each company car may be associated with a single employee, there is no tie up between the entity tables *at this stage*.

ie. There is nothing in:

the employee table to say which car is owned

or the company car table to say who owns it.

This comes later in the analysis.

2.4 Key Fields For Each Table

Each row in each data table *must* be unique.

If there is a chance that two rows may be the same a new attribute must be added to make each row unique.

Eg. The ID number in the employee table.

Any column in which all entries are unique is called a **key** field. A table must have:

either: A single key field column.

or: A combination of columns that together form a unique key, and is known as a multiple key.

Examples of single key fields are:

1. The ID number in the employee table.
2. The Reg.No. in the company car table.

An example of a multiple key would be:

Suppose all employees must belong to one of a number of recognised trade unions...

... the union membership number alone is not unique...

... but a combination of union name and the union membership number is unique, so these columns would provide a multiple key.

In such instances a new single key field is often introduced for convenience.

2.5 Should an Attribute be an Entity?

Hint 1 : Variable numbers of an Attribute

Check the attributes of all entities -

Are there variable numbers of an attribute?

Eg. An item may have several different colours.

If so then make the attribute a separate entity.

Otherwise there will be blank fields in the data base.

This can give unexpected entities such as Colour.

If an item can have several colours,

and different items have different numbers of colours

then the colour must be a separate entity.

But: If all the items had multiple colours but each had the same number of colours there would be no need of a separate colour entity.

2.6 Should an Attribute be an Entity?

Hint 2 : Optional Attributes

Check the attributes of all entities -

Is any attribute optional?

Eg. The passport number attribute of a person entity.

If so, then strictly speaking it should be made an entity.

Otherwise there will be blank fields in the data base.

In practice if most occurrences of this entity have this attribute (eg. most people have a passport.) then it is commonly left as an attribute.

This is a compromise . . .

. . . simplicity is being gained at the expense of wasted space in the data base.

2.7 Should an Attribute be an Entity?

Hint 3 : Attributes With Attributes

Check the attributes of all entities -

Has any attribute got an attribute of its own?

Eg. A person entity may have a car type and a car length as attributes . . .

. . . in this case the car length is really an attribute of the car type.

If an attribute has an attribute of its own then it should be made into a separate entity.

Otherwise the attributes are interdependent and there is a risk that the data base could become inconsistent.

Eg. A persons car type may be changed with the user forgetting to change the car length . . .

. . . this could lead to two people with the same car type but with different car lengths.

2.8 Should an Attribute be an Entity?

Hint 4 : Repeated, Long Text Attributes

Check the attributes of all entities -

> *Is any long text attribute likely to be repeated for different occurrences of the entity?*

ie. More than one person may have the same car type, such as "Ford Escort Estate".

If there are many repeats

or the text is long

then there can be a significant space saving by making this attribute into a separate entity referenced by an id number.

ie. A separate table should be created with the text and an associated identity number . . .

> . . . other tables will then refer to the id number rather than the text itself.

2.9 Should an Attribute be an Entity?

Hint 5 : Text Attributes Used In Matchings

Check the attributes of all entities -

Is any text attribute likely to be tested for matching entries?

Even if the text is short with only a few repeats . . .

if tests may be made for matching entries,

then it should be a separate entity.

Eg. A TOWN attribute could have any of the entries:

```
Leicester Leics  Leic   Leics. Leic.
LEICESTER LEICS  LEIC   LEICS. LEIC.
```

This is OK if it is only used as part of an address. . .

But . . . if matching on the name is to be done, (eg. to list all people from Leicester)

then entries may be missed!

If the field is made a separate entity

then each name would be stored once only with only one representation.

2.10 Single Instance Entities

Some entities by the nature of the way they are handled can only ever have one instance.

Eg. Finance Office, The Government, The Car Pool

Other entities may have all instances considered to be identical with no need to distinguish between them.

Eg. Backing Store, Member of Public, Train

- **These do not qualify as proper entities!**
- **They should not appear in any entity diagram!**
- **They will not appear in any data table!**

To include these single entities in any entity diagrams would:

1. Increase the entity diagram size and hence increase the diagram's complexity.
2. Produce no useful outcome as no table needs to be derived to store data about them.

ie. Single instance entities hinder rather than help the understanding of the system data.

In other words - forget all single instance entities!

2.11 Step 2 - Determine the Relationships

These can be represented in a diagram using

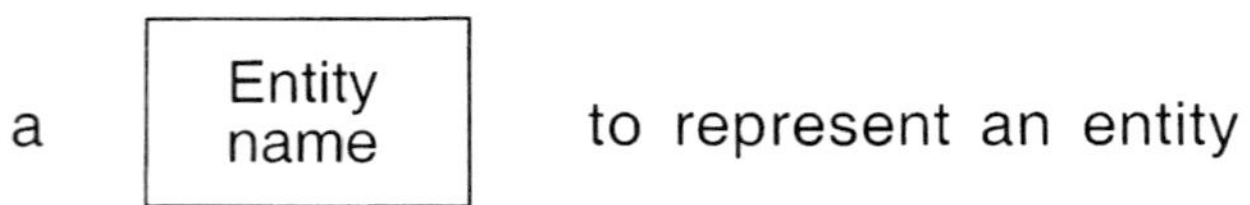

with connecting lines to represent relationships in the form:

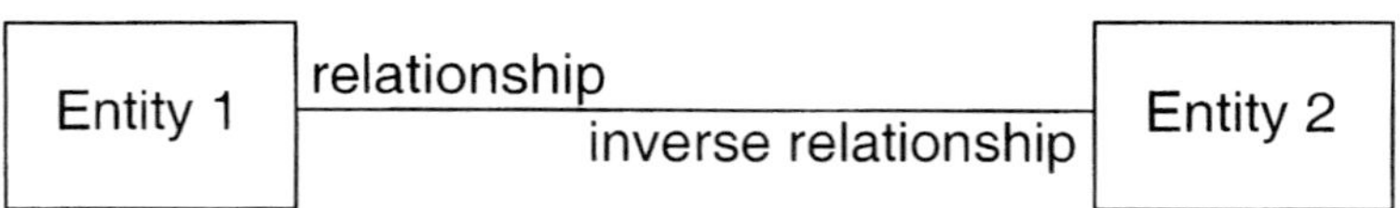

The relationship labelling can be above or below the connecting line.

For example:

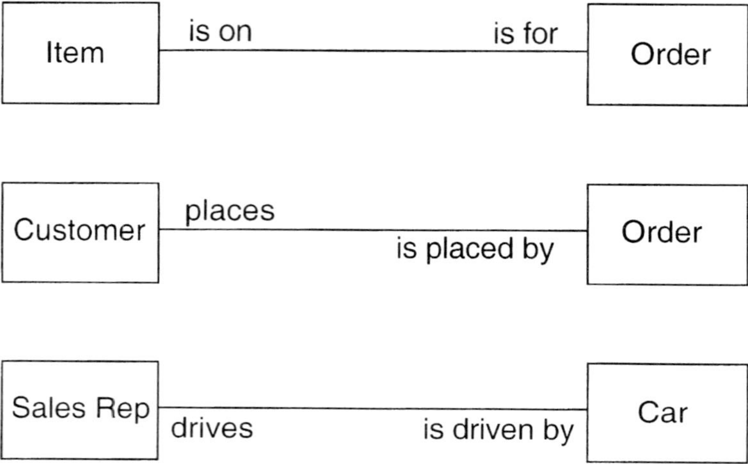

2.12 Processes Verses Relationships

Time considerations are largely ignored in entity relationship analysis.....

.... but the entity relationship diagram produced must be accurate for any *instant* in time.

Eg. The "relationship"

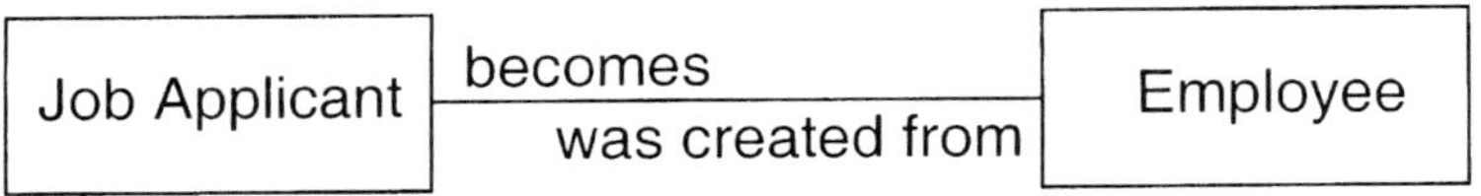

is ***not a valid relationship*** because:

1. At any one instant in time a person cannot be both a job applicant and an employee.

2. At any one instant in time there is no connection between any of the current job applicants and any of the current employees.

ie. "becomes/was created from" is a process....

....not a relationship!

2.13 Positioning the Relationship Name

To save space on an entity diagram:

- It is not necessary to put both the relationship and its inverse on the connecting line, providing the meaning is clear.

- The relationship name can be put centrally if the relationship direction is obvious.

eg. A Car would not drive a Sales Rep so the meaning and direction of the relationship is obvious:

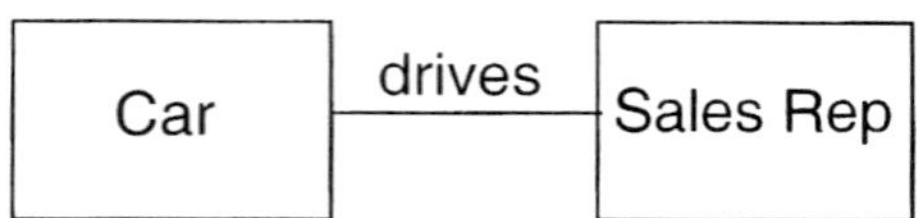

If the direction of the relationship is not obvious the relationship wording should be nearer the "from" entity:

Eg.

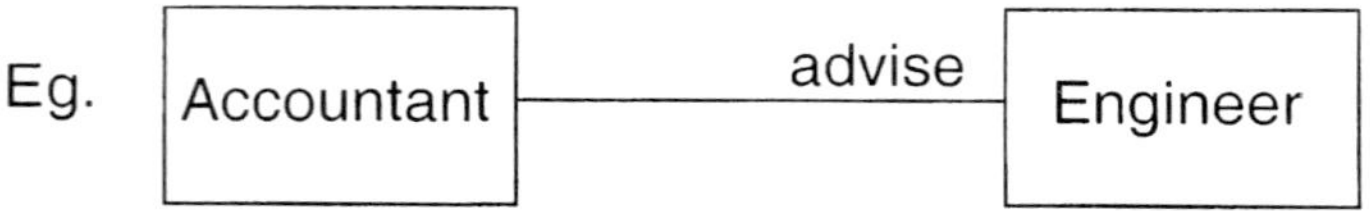

This shows that the engineers advise the accountants, not the other way round.

2.14 Alternative Notations

Some entity diagram notations involve a ◇ to label the relationship:

But this notation may make the diagrams more cluttered.

Some notations (eg.SSADM) allow the naming of the relationship to be omitted altogether ....

.... but this is **NOT** recommended.

It is important because there may be more than one relationship which will lead, eventually, to more than one data table.

Eg.

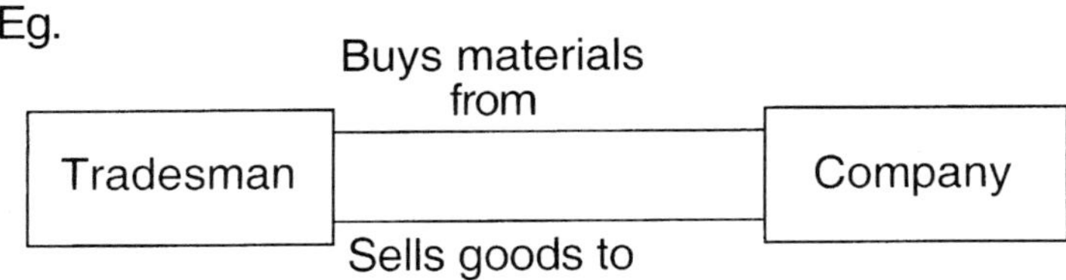

Such multiple relationships can easily be missed if the relationships are not named.

2.15 Merging Entities

The attributes and relationships may show that some entities are very similar.

ie.
- The number of attributes is the same.
- The types of attributes are the same.
- They relationships with other entities are the same (or nearly the same).

Eg. Two entities are EC Worker and Non EC Worker

Each has attributes: ID Number, Job Title, Salary

Each has relationships: *belongs to* Department
and *works on* Project

The Non EC Worker also has the relationship:
Non EC Worker*must have a* Work Permit

These could be merged into one entity, Worker, if:

1. The Work Permit relationship becomes optional.
   ie. Workers *may have a* Work Permit.

2. The attributes indicate the type of worker.

   This could mean either:

   1. adding a new "worker type" column

   or 2. Making an existing column specify the worker type (Eg. Only Non EC workers have ID numbers > 1000)

2.16 Should Two Entities be Merged?

There is no fixed rule over whether or not entities should be merged....

.... it depends on how the entity tables will be used.

If the information to be derived will usually require putting data from both tables together

then the table should be merged.

Eg. For the EC / Non EC Workers example, operations such as:

- totalling salaries for each department
- seeing which engineers work on a certain project

.... would be better served by a single merged table.

Whereas operations such as:

- checking who's work permit will soon expire
- allocating only EC Workers to defence projects

.... would be better served by separate entity tables.

It is for the database designer to judge which is the most appropriate data structure for each separate application.

2.17 Reflective Entity Relationships

It is possible for entities to have a relationship with other entities of the same type.

eg. Person *is a friend of* person

and, if a sales item such as a "crate of wine" contains other sales items such as "bottle of wine"

Item *contains* item

These are known as **reflective** relationships and are shown on the entity diagram as follows:

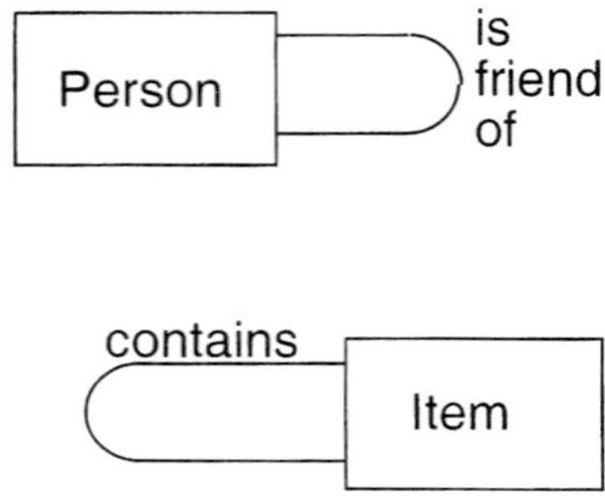

Note : Reflective relationships are relatively rare....

... frequently it is more convenient to split the entity. Eg. "Container item" and "Internal item"

2.18 Step 3 - Combine into One Diagram

No one entity appears in more than one place:

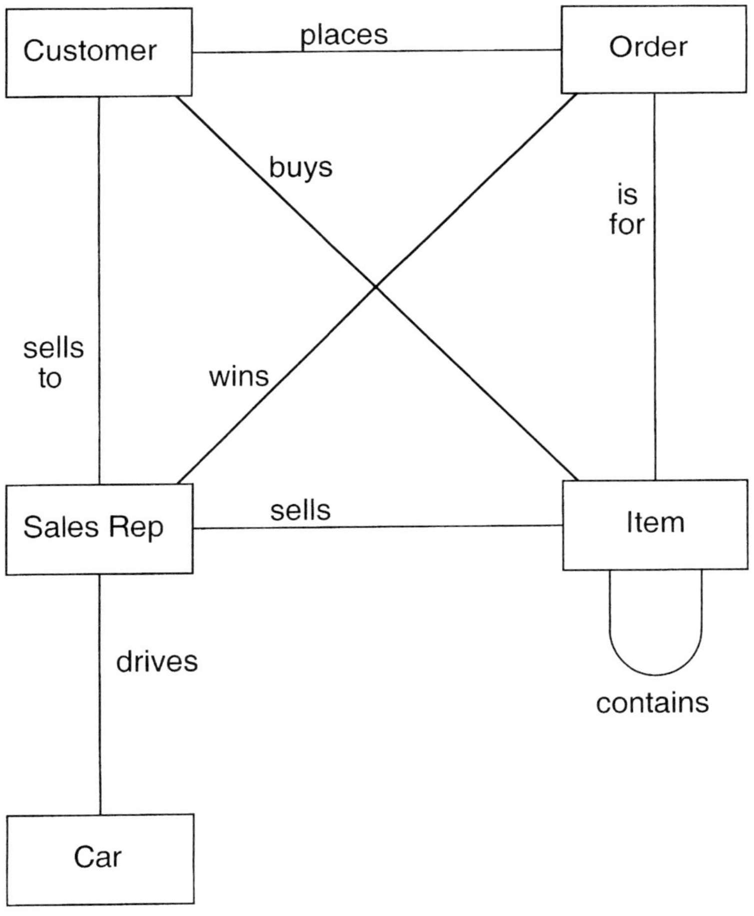

CHAPTER 3

Adding Detail to the Entity Relationship Diagram

Contents Page

3.1 Dependent Entities

Each instance of *dependent* entity only exists because of an instance of another, different entity.

These are sometimes called "detail" or "weak" entities, each being like an attribute of the other "master" or "strong" entity.

There are two types of dependent entities:

1. A detail entity where each instance is associated with only one of the master entity.

   Eg. A company car entity where each and every car is allocated to just one sales rep entity.

   Instances of detail entity cease to exist when the corresponding master entity no longer exists....

   ie. The car is sold when the sales rep leaves the company.

2. A detail entity table where each instance may be associated with several instances of the master entity.

   Eg. A job title entity where each title may be associated with several employee entities.

   The detail entity would be deleted when the last corresponding master entity is deleted.

   ie. There are no job titles kept for non existent employees.

3.2 Showing Dependent Entities

Both types of dependent entity are shown with a double outline box:

eg.

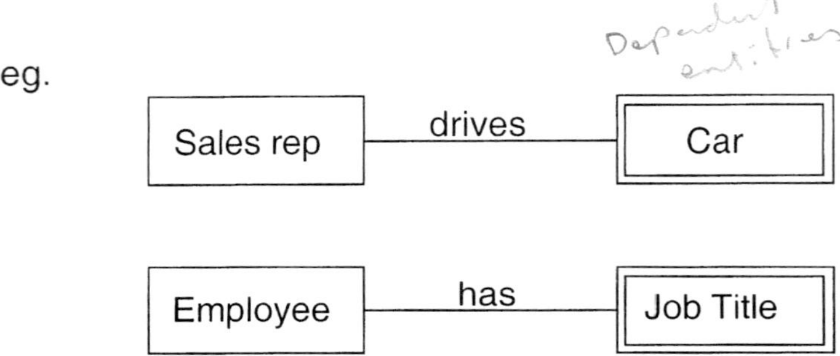

It is not essential to show dependent entities any differently to other entities as the data table structure derived will be no different.

But .... knowing the dependent entities does enable the corresponding data tables to be handled correctly when the master entity table is modified.

Some entity relation diagram notations allow for *all* attributes of an entity to be shown in circular boxes:

eg.

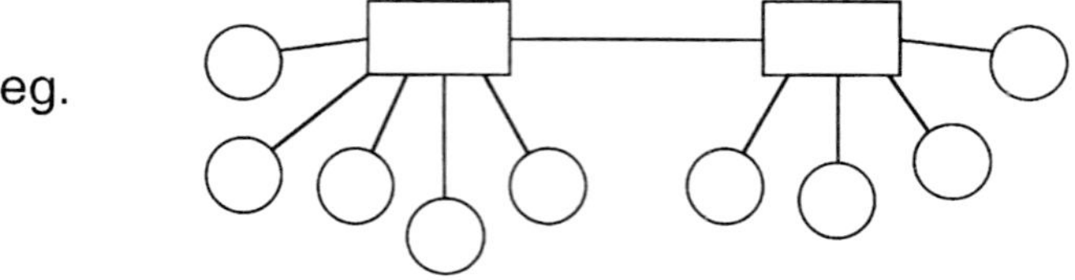

.... but this is not recommended as it leads to cluttered diagrams that are hard to follow.

3.3 Classifying the Relationships

A relationship may be:

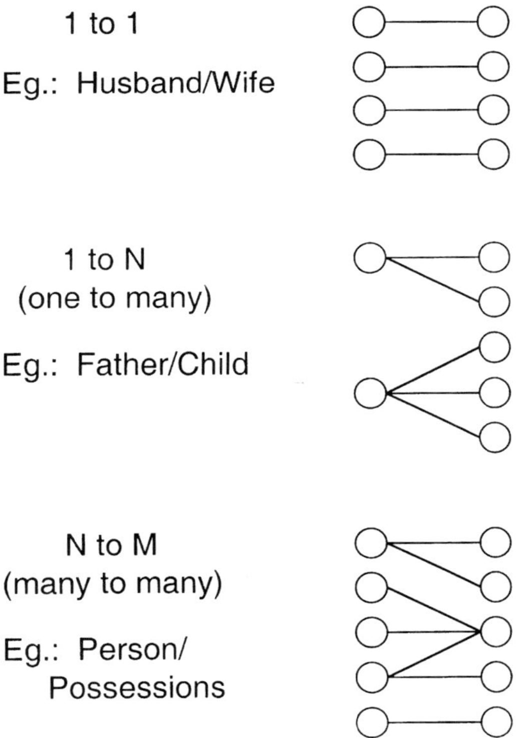

These classifications may be represented in the form:

Father **1** is parent of **N** Child

3.4 Alternative Notations

One to many relationships

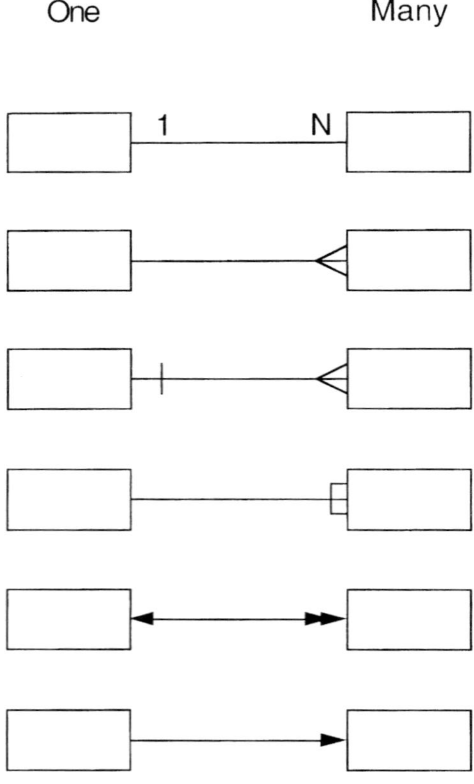

3.5 Obligatory and Non Obligatory Relationships

If membership of a relationship is optional for an entity it may be shown by:

Eg.

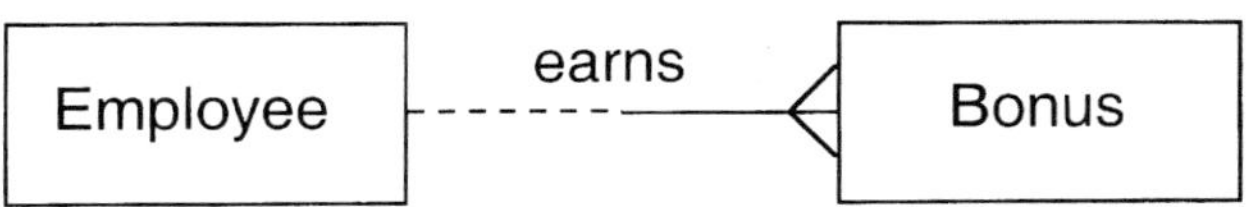

Some employees get one or more bonuses but some don't.
Every bonus is given to an employee.

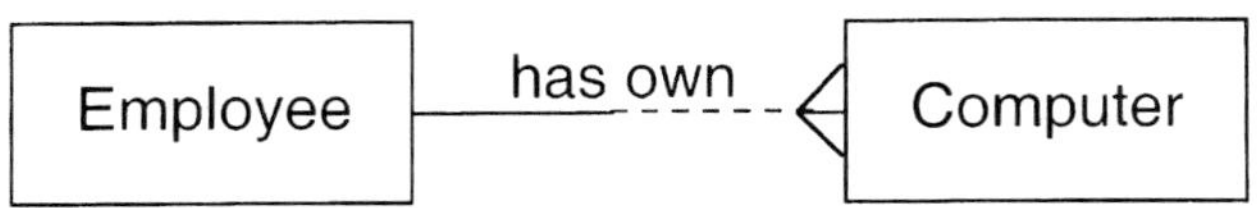

Every employee has one or more computers.
Some computers are not assigned to any particular employee.

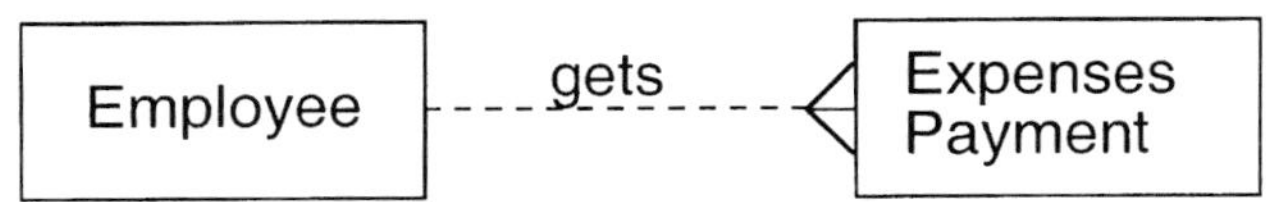

Some employees will get one or more expenses payments but some will not.

Some expenses payments will go to employees but some will not (eg. get paid to consultants).

3.6 Using a Range of Membership to Show Optionality

If an entity must belong to a relationship it can be considered to be connected to a minimum of one of the other entity.

If it's membership of the relationship is optional then it is connected to a minimum of zero of the other entities.

A range giving minimum as well as maximum order of membership can be shown to indicate optionality:

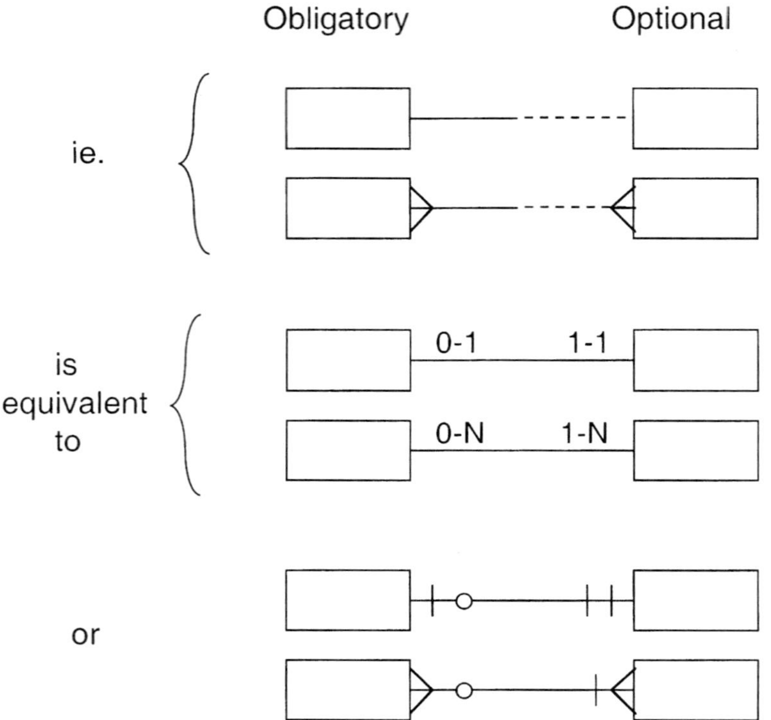

3.7 Ambiguity in Notations for Optionality

A circle can also be used to indicate optionality:

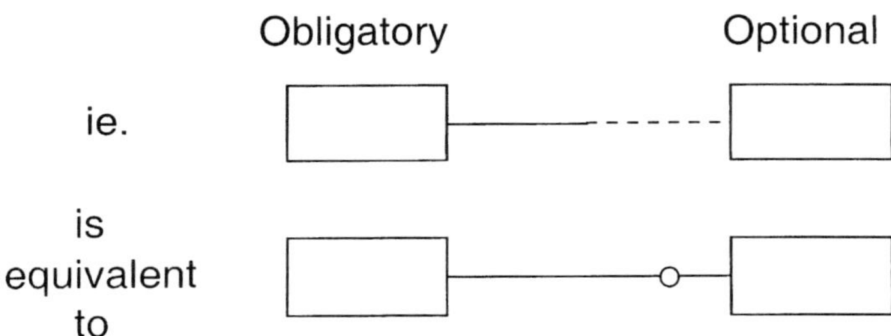

But a circle is sometimes used to indicate a minimum of zero with no corresponding lines to indicate a minimum of one:

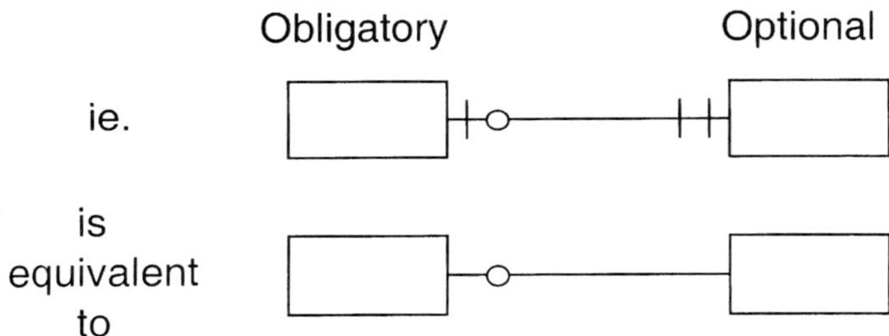

This means the diagram can be interpreted either way round!

Therefore, if a circle is to be used *always* put a key to make your notation absolutely clear!

3.8 Time Considerations for Optionality

The entity relationship diagram must be true for any *instant* in time....

ie. it must allow for even *short lived* situations.

This can make membership of some relationships optional even if intuitively this would not be the case.

Eg. If **all** sales reps drive company cars ....

but it may take a few weeks to arrange a company car when they first start ....

then the relationship must be shown as:

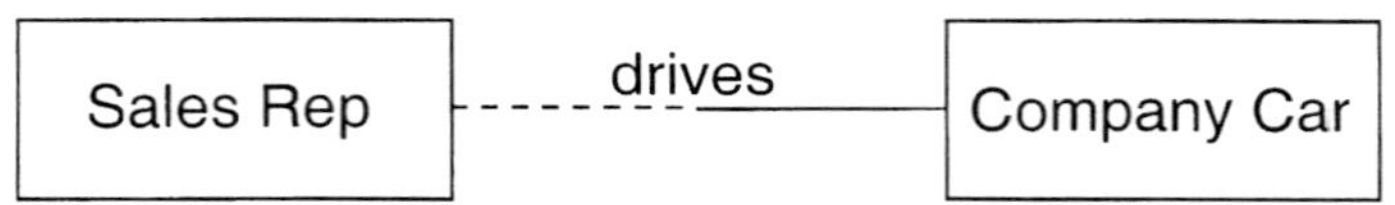

ie. At any instant in time there may be some sales reps without cars ....

.... so for the sales rep the relationship is considered to be *optional*.

3.9 *Either - Or* Relationships

Mutually exclusive alternative options are shown by an arc crossing each relationship line.

Suppose
- *all* sales reps drive cars
- when they start they drive a hire car
- this is then replaced by a company car

ie. All sales reps drive *either* a hire car *or* a company car.

This is shown by:

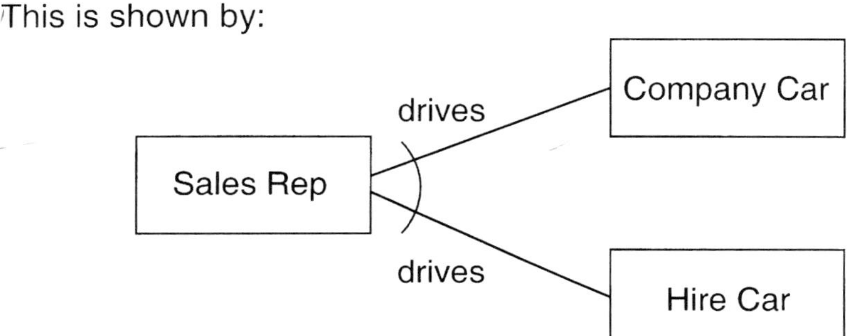

A dashed line is used *only* if sales reps may exist who drive *neither* a hire car *nor* a company car.

ie:

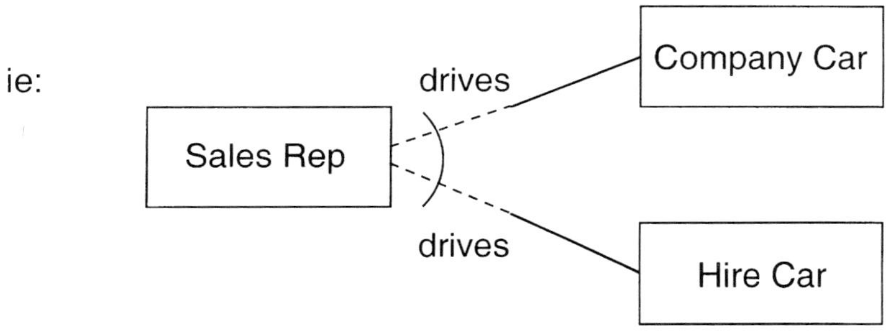

3.10 The Full Entity Relationship Diagram

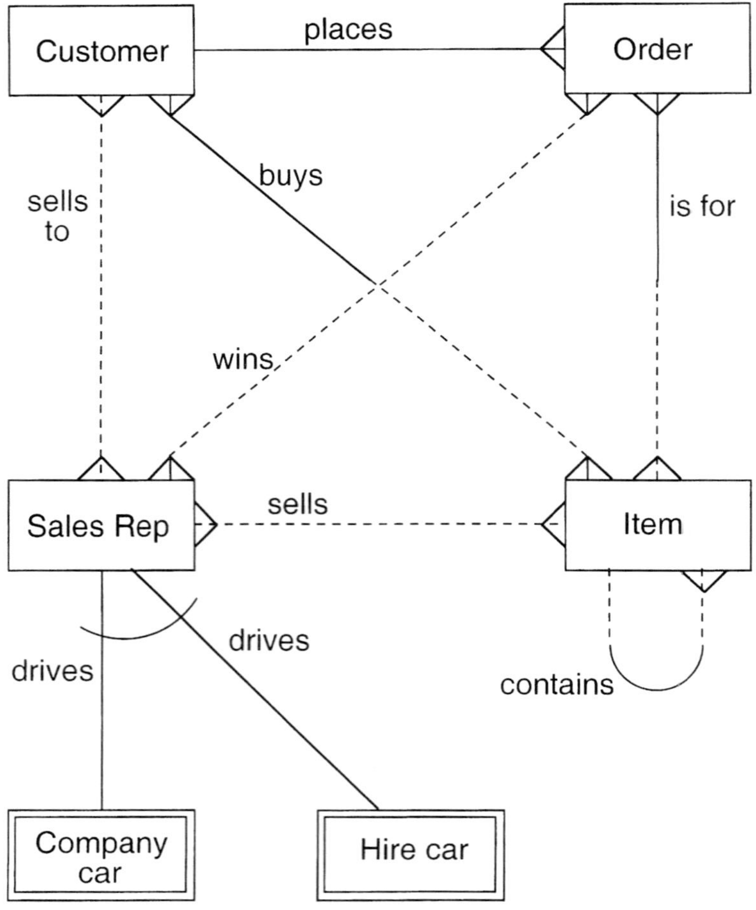

CHAPTER 4

Rationalising the Entity Relationship Diagram

Contents | Page

4.1 Eliminating Redundant Relationships

Some relationships duplicate information shown in other relationships:

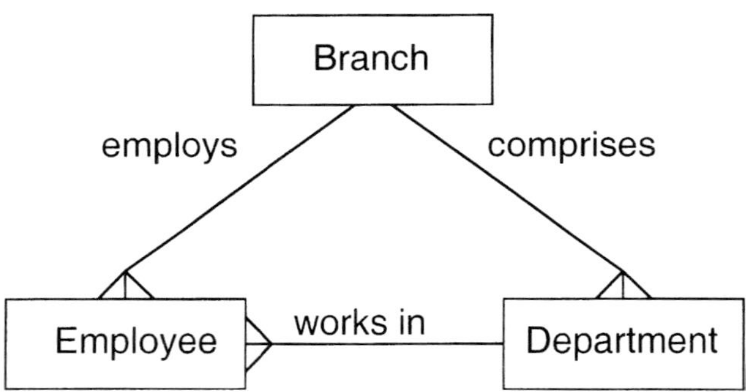

The fact that an employee works in a branch of the company follows from:

1. All employees work in a department
2. All departments form part of a branch

ie. The branch - employee relationship is redundant and can be eliminated:

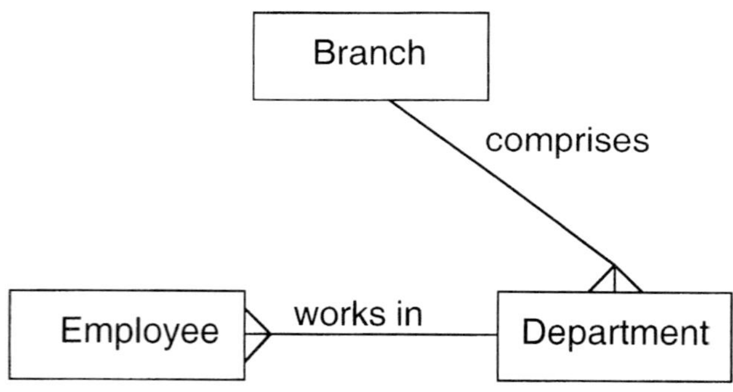

4.2 Ambiguity When Eliminating Relationships

Care must be taken that there is no loss in information when eliminating relationships:

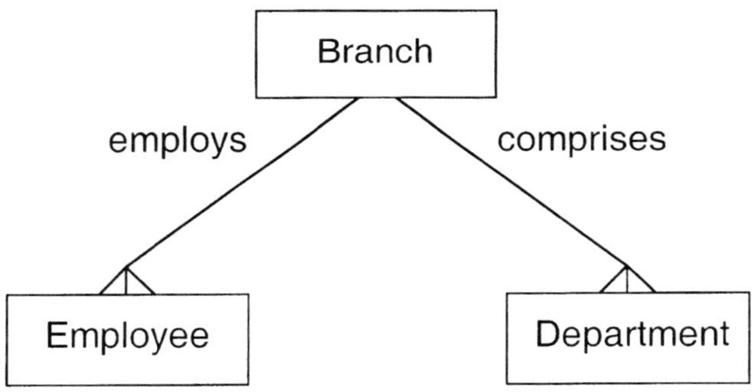

The above at first appears to have eliminated a redundant relationship - but which department does each employee belong to?

Care must be taken not to model a relationship with an indirect connection of the type N:... + ...:N such as:

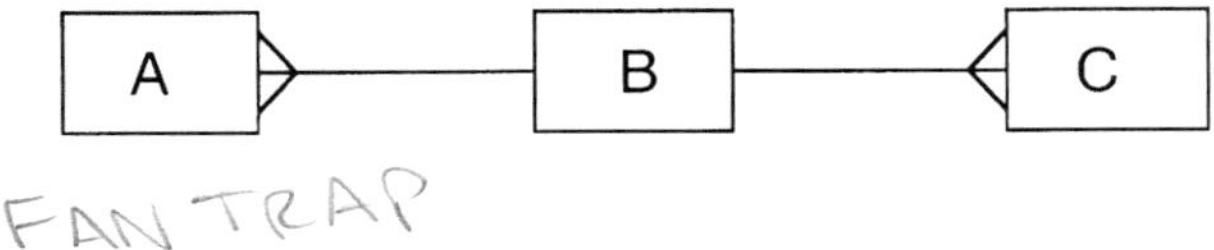

This gives ambiguous information about how A is connected to C.

This is known as the "fan trap" as there is a "fan" (ie. a <) at both ends.

4.3 Loss of Connection When Eliminating Relationships

If some of the connections are optional then care must be taken to avoid loosing connections when eliminating relationships.

This is known as the "chasm trap".

For example:

If
some branch employees were not allocated to any particular department (eg. directors)

ie.
the employees membership of the "works in" relationship is optional

then
the branch - employee relationship is **not** redundant.

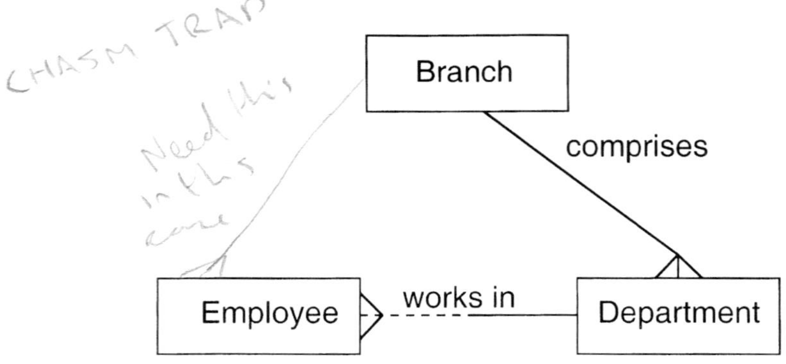

For some employees the connection to the branch is now lost!

4.4 The Entity Relationship Diagram After Eliminating Redundant Relationships

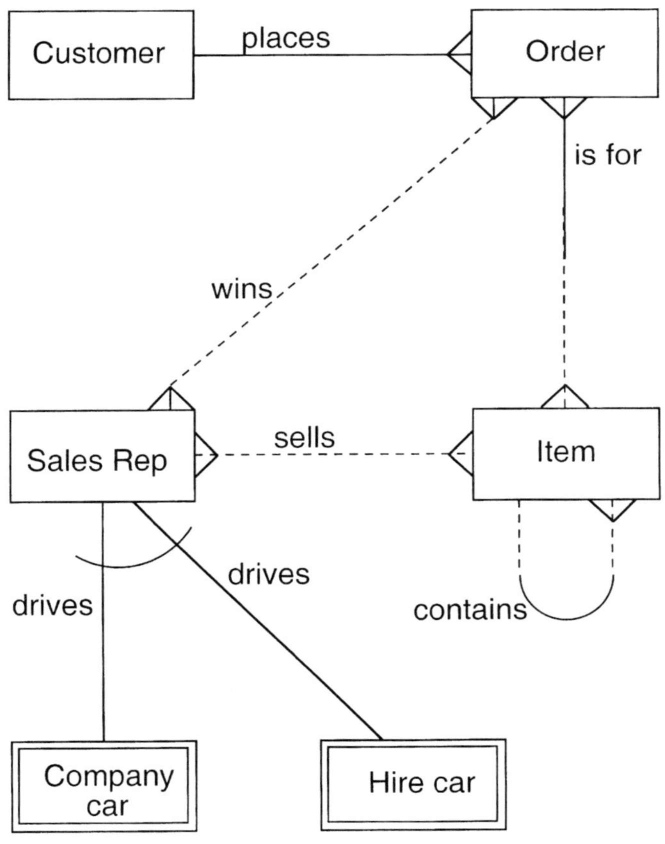

4.5 Finding New Dependent Entities

Once the entity relationship diagram has been simplified it will often reveal new dependent entities.

If any entity has a relationship with only one other entity and it must belong to that relationship ....

.... then it can be considered to be a dependent entity:

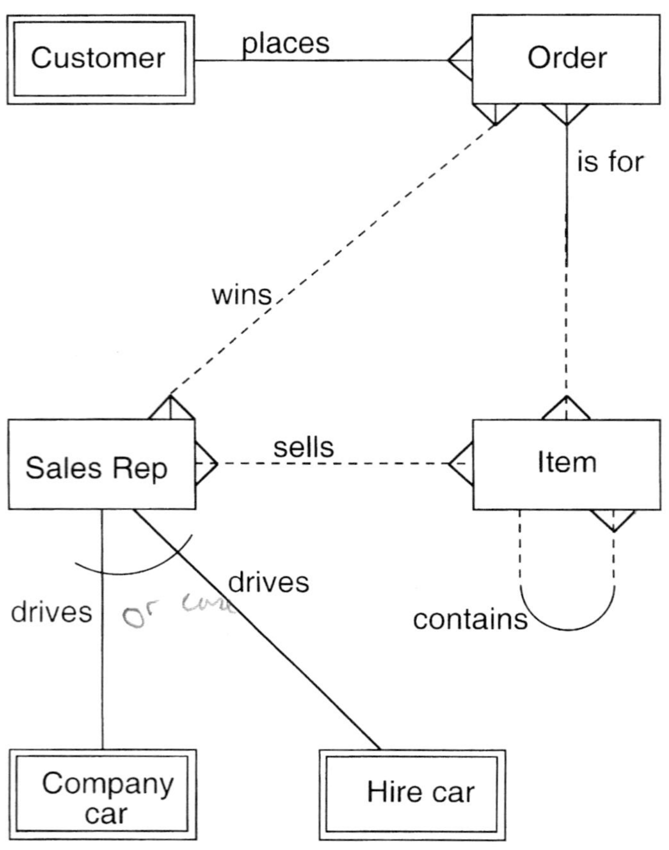

4.6 Checking To See If The Relationships Tell Us Everything We Need To Know

Eg In the example we have:

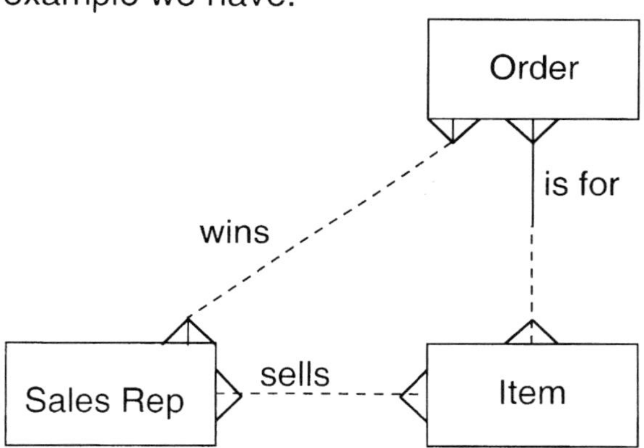

- We know which sales reps have sold what items.

  Eg. Fred and Flo may both have sold items A and B on various different customer's orders.

- We know which sales reps have won what orders.

  Eg. Fred and Flo may both be responsible for order X.

- We know which items are on what orders.

  Eg. Order X may be for items A and B.

But We don't know who managed to get each individual item onto each order.

ie. Did Fred sell A and Flo sell B on order X or was it vice-versa?

4.7 3-Way Relationships

Circular relationships that cannot be eliminated as in the Sales Rep - Order - Item relationships may need to be represented as a 3-way relationship:

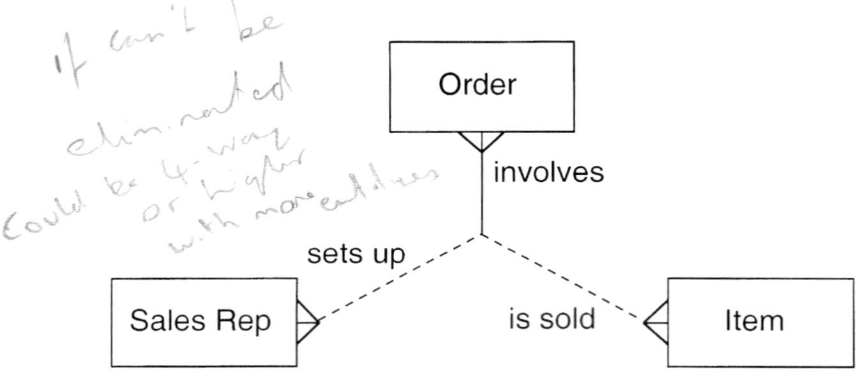

Unfortunately it is difficult to represent this type of relationship in words!

Note:

1. It may not be possible to create a 3-way relationship. Not all cycles of relationship pairs can be represented this way.

2. It is theoretically possible to have 4-way or even more complex multi-way relationships - though these are rare in practice.

4.8 When Not To Introduce A Multi-way Relationship

This 3-way relationship should only be created if it provides information that is needed.

Eg. In the sales rep - order - item example do we need to know who is responsible for what on each order?

If not, the relationship should be left as 3 pairs as before.

Why?

Although it may look simpler there may be a lot of data needed to define a 3-way relationship.

Eg. If there are 10 sales reps, 10 orders and 10 items then ....

a 3-way relationship represents a possible 10*10*10 = 1000 possible combinations ....

whereas, the 3 relationship pairs represent only 10*10 + 10*10 + 10*10 = 300 possible combinations.

Each situation must be considered separately to determine which is the most accurate and useful way to model the real relationships.

4.9 Looking for "Hidden" Entities

Many-Many Relationships can be difficult to handle - as will be seen later when special relationship tables will be needed.

It may be useful to invent another entity between these many-many entities to:

- Assist the understanding of these relationships
- Enable them to be handled more easily.

ie.

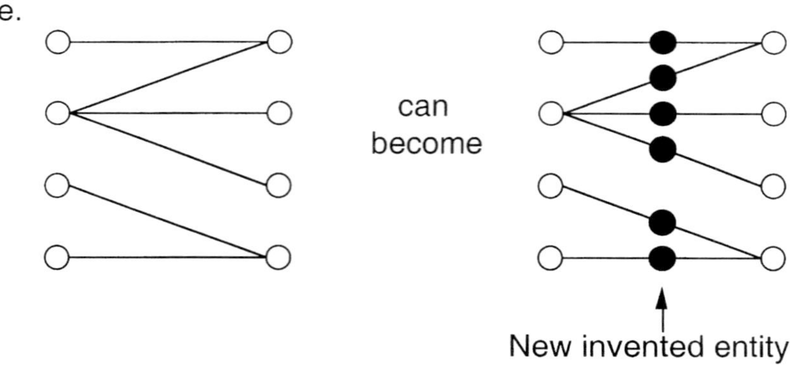

This new entity will be an obligatory 'N' of a 1 to N relationship with each of the other two entities.

When considered, this new entity may turn out to represent something meaningful.

In which case:

- It may have attributes of its own
- It may have relationships with other entities

4.10 Example of a "Discovered" Entity

If a 3-way has not been created in the sales entity relationship diagram there is still the many-many relationship:

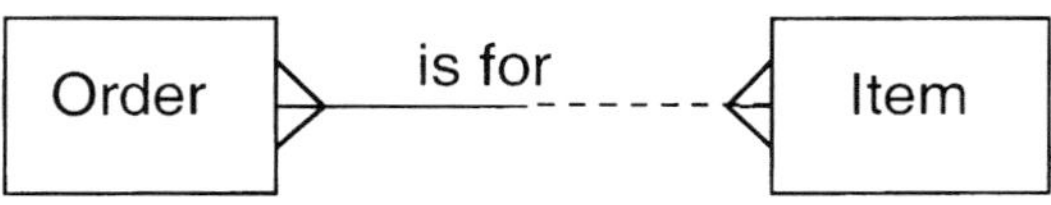

Introducing "Sale", meaning the sale of one type of item on one order gives:

There is now two 1:N relationships with the new entity connected to one and only one of each of the original two entities.

But note - This new entity will not make any difference to the data tables that will be derived from the diagram unless it is found to have:

either: its own attributes

or: its own relationships with other entities

These make the new entity worth creating.

Note : Although this entity is not directly "tangible" itself, there are associated things which are very real - eg. the bill!

4.11 New Relationships for a Discovered Entity

Once a new entity is discovered it may be found that other relationships to this entity exist and these may lead to other relationships becoming redundant:

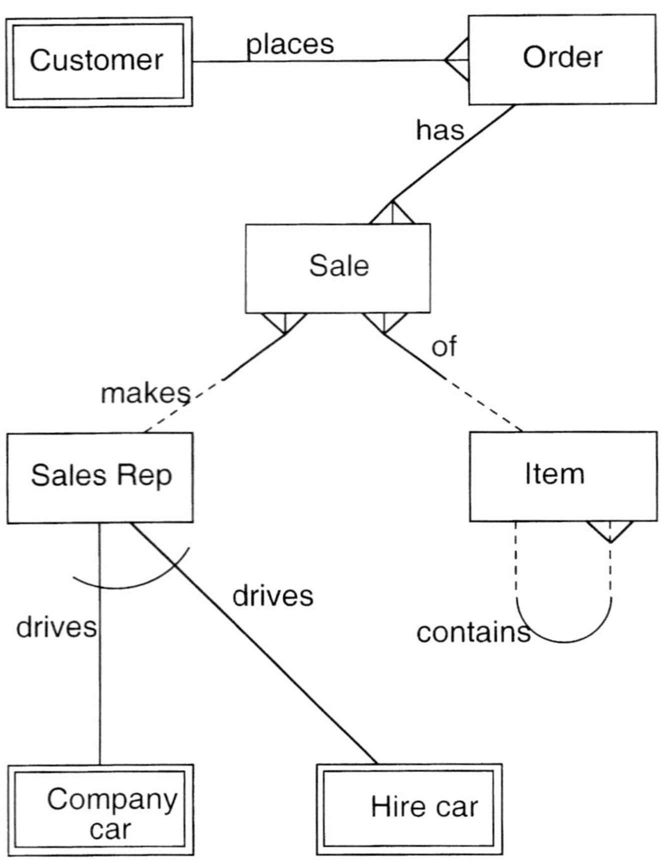

4.12 3-Way Relationships and Discovered Entities

3-way and other multi-way relationships may be represented by a discovered entity - this may assist in the understanding of the relationship.

Eg. A 3-way relationship created for the "Sales rep - Order - Item" cycle could also give a discovered entity called "Sale":

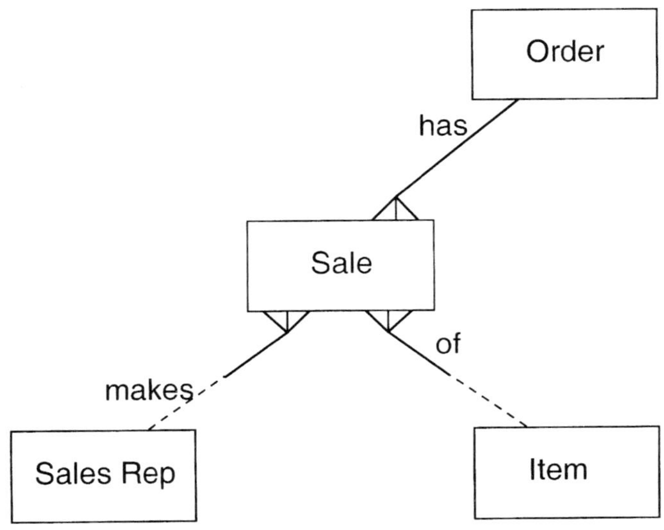

This is exactly the same diagram as created when discovering an entity for the 2-way relationship and then finding a third relationship for the new entity.

ie. There may be equally valid alternative routes to derive the final entity relationship diagram.

CHAPTER 5

Creating the Entity Relationship Data Tables

Contents | Page

5.1 Creating Entity Data Dictionary Entries

The data dictionary is a description of the layout for each data table in the system with:

- A separate table for each entity type.
- A separate row for each instance of that type of entity in the entity table.
- A separate column for each entity attribute.
- A unique table key based on one or more of the associated columns.

Note: If a key consists of two or more fields, it may be convenient to invent a new field to act as a key, such as an identity number.

Eg.

Item Table

Item Code	Description	Manufacturer	Price
P1234	Pogo Stick	Bouncy Toys plc	£10
801-bd	"Bonzo" doll	LoadaRubbish ltd	£5
18/zap	Lazer gun	Futuristics UK ltd	£50
BossMk2	Inflatable HoD	Gas-filler plc	£1000

Order Table

Order ID	Order Date	Delivered?	Discount
2001	10/11/92	yes	0%
2002	01/02/93	no	10%
2003	01/02/93	partly	5%

5.2 Creating the Relationship Links

Method 1 : Merging the Entity Tables

Applicable to:
Obligatory 1 to 1 Relationships

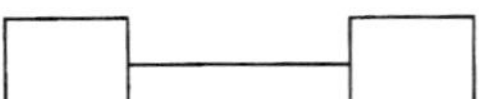

Eg. For the relationship:

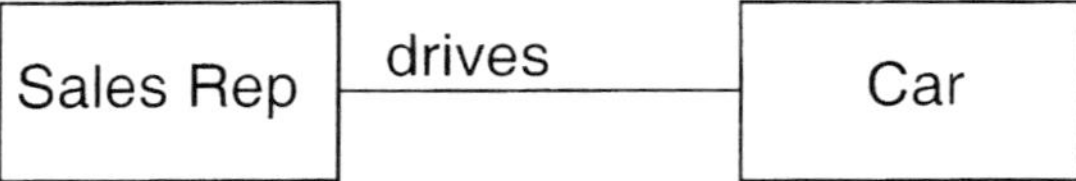

with entity tables:

Rep.ID -> Name, Sales, Commission
Reg.No. -> Make, Model, Miles

If every sales rep drives a car
and every car is driven by a sales rep
then the tables can be combined into:

Rep.ID -> Name, Sales, Commission, Reg.No.,
Make, Model, Miles

Alternatively the Reg.No. could be the key field.

Notice that any attribute mistakenly designated as a separate entity will be absorbed into the appropriate entity table at this point.

5.3 Compromise Use of Method 1

Applicable to:

Obligatory-Optional 1 to 1 Relationships

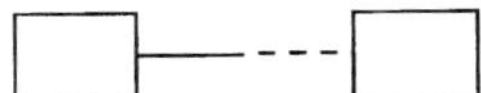

If every car is driven by a sales rep
but a sales rep does not necessarily drive a car
then the tables can be merged to:

Rep.ID -> Name, Sales, Commission,
Reg.No., Make, Model, Miles.

Note: This is bending the rules with the disadvantage that:

- There will be some null fields in the database, this wastes space.
- Some fields will be interdependent in that, if any of the fields Reg.No., Make, Model and Miles are empty for a particular sales rep, then all of these fields must be empty.

Whether or not such a compromise is desirable will depend on the proportion of null fields in the table.

If there are too many null fields it would be better to use method 2 to create the relationship link.

5.4 Create the Relationship Links

Method 2 : Adding the Key of One Table to the Other

Applicable to:

Obligatory-Optional 1 to 1 Relationships

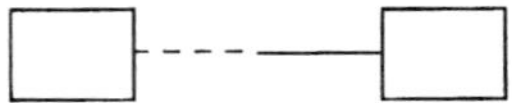

1 to N Relationships Obligatory for the 'N' Entity

In this case the key field of the optional or '1' entity table is added to the obligatory or 'N' entity table.

If every car is driven by one sales rep
but a sales rep does not necessarily drive a car
or a sales rep may drive more than one car
then the relationship can be modelled by:

Rep.ID -> Name, Sales, Commission
Reg.No. -> Make, Model, Miles, Rep.ID

Note the field(s) containing the key for a different table is known as a **foreign key**.

eg. Rep.ID is a foreign key in the Car table.

5.5 Compromise Use of Method 2

Applicable to:

Optional-Optional 1 to 1 Relationships

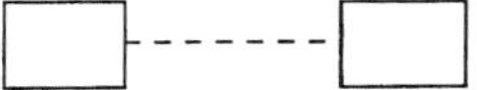

1 to N Relationships Optional for the 'N' Entity

If a car is <u>not necessarily</u> driven by a sales rep
and a sales rep does not necessarily drive a car
or a sales rep may drive more than one car
then the relationship can be modelled by:

Rep.ID -> Name, Sales, Commission
Reg.No. -> Make, Model, Miles, Rep.ID

But Note: This is once again bending the rules giving some null fields in the Rep.ID field in the Car table - and this wastes space.

Whether or not such a compromise is desirable will depend on the proportion of null fields in the table.

If there are too many cars not driven by sales reps it would be better to create a relationship table as in method 3 to create the relationship link.

5.6 Create the Relationship Links

Method 3 : Creating a Relationship Table

Applicable to:

Optional-Optional 1 to 1 Relationships

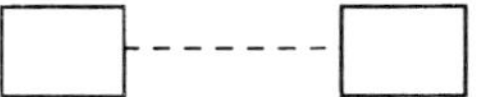

1 to N Relationships Optional for the 'N' Entity

N to N Relationships, Optional or Obligatory

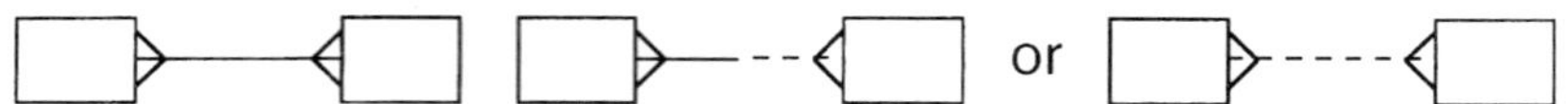

If a car is not necessarily driven by a sales rep
or a car may be driven by more than one sales rep

and a sales rep does not necessarily drive a car
or a sales rep may drive more than one car

then a Relationship Table can relate the entities with

- Fields (columns) corresponding to the key fields of the related entities.
- A separate entry (row) for each instance of a relationship between the entities.

N.B. This is the **only way** to model many to many relationships

5.7 Example of a Relationship Table

A relationship table will only have columns corresponding to the 2 keys of the 2 entities it relates ....

.... this usually gives a table with just 2 columns.

Eg. A many to many relationship between the Order and Item entities would give:

Order-Item Relationship Table

Order ID	Item Code
2001	P1234
2001	18/zap
2002	BossMk2
2003	801-bd
2003	18/zap
2003	BossMk2

There is one row in this table for every order-item relation.

Neither column is unique .... the two columns make a multiple key.

3-way relationships would have a further column(s) corresponding to the key of the third entity:

Order-Item-Sales Rep 3-way Relationship Table

Order ID	Item Code	First Name	Second Name
2001	P1234	Fred	Bloggs
2001	18/zap	Joe	Smith
2002	BossMk2	Fred	Bloggs

5.8 Discovered Entity Tables

A discovered entity will have as its key a combination of fields that correspond to the key fields of the entities it was "discovered" between.

If a discovered entity has no further attributes of its own then the resulting table has no further columns...

.... but this is exactly the same as the relationship table that would have existed had the entity not been discovered!

This shows that unless:

1. The entity has attributes of its own

or 2. The entity is needed as further entities will relate to it

then "discovering" an entity gives no advantage.

In the example of the "Sale" being a discovered entity a possible extra attribute may be the number of each item on the order:

"Sale" Discovered Entity Table

Order ID	Item Code	First Name	Second Name	Number
2001	P1234	Fred	Bloggs	12
2001	18/zap	Joe	Smith	100
2002	BossMk2	Fred	Bloggs	1

5.9 Either-Or Relationships

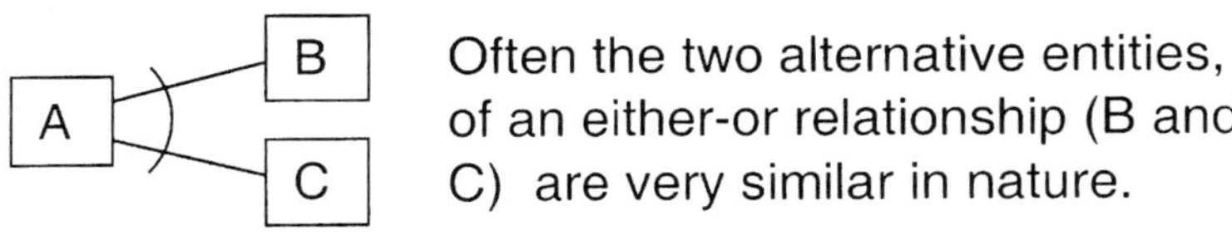

Often the two alternative entities, of an either-or relationship (B and C) are very similar in nature.

Eg. Company Cars and Hire Cars are clearly similar.

If the data record for each entity is also similar, (the entity tables have the same number and type of columns)

then

- the entity tables can be combined into one
- an extra column should define the entity type

Eg Suppose both the Company Car and the Hire Car entities had attributes:

Reg.No. -> Make, Model, Miles

The tables should be combined into one with an extra Boolean field to signify whether the car was a company car or hire car:

Reg.No. -> Make, Model, Miles, Car type

The entity diagram can then be revised and redrawn and the associated tables derived accordingly.

5.10 Handling Either-or Relationships as Options

If the alternative entities do not have records of identical format.

then it is possible to treat the relationship in exactly the same way as optional relationships.

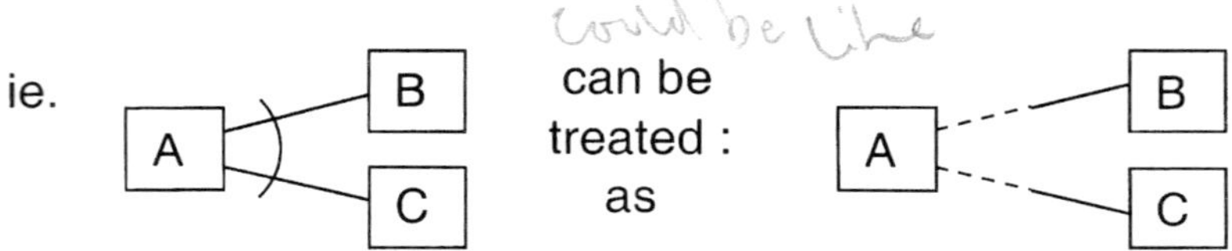

But:

1. This hides the either-or nature of the relationship

2. The resulting tables would not prevent an 'A' entity having a relationship with both 'B' and 'C'.

However the relationships ***must*** be treated as optional relationships if either B or C are the 'N' entity of a 1 to N or N to N relationship:

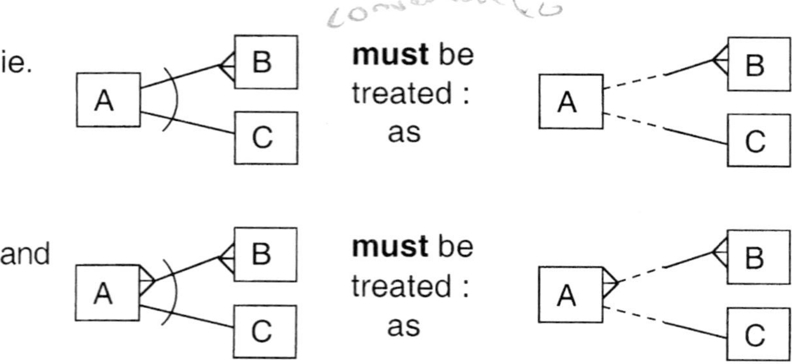

5.11 Shared Foreign Key Fields

If the alternative fields in an either-or relationship are both the '1' end of a 1 to 1 or 1 to N relationship

and

the key fields of both are of the same format

and

the keys are distinct from each other

then

the keys of both may be stored in the same field in the linking entity table.

ie. In the case of

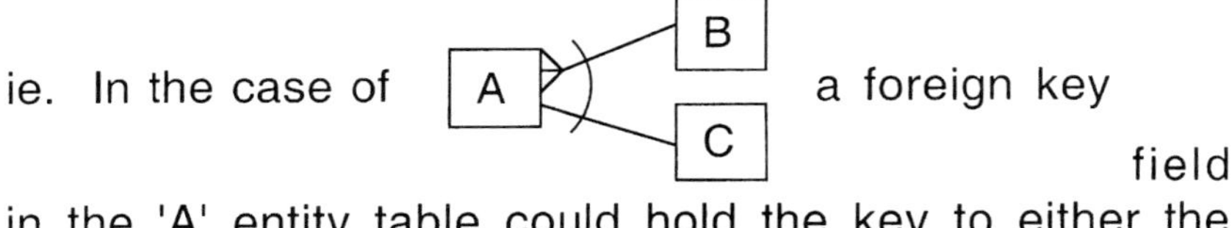

a foreign key field in the 'A' entity table could hold the key to either the 'B' table or the 'C' table.

And in the case of

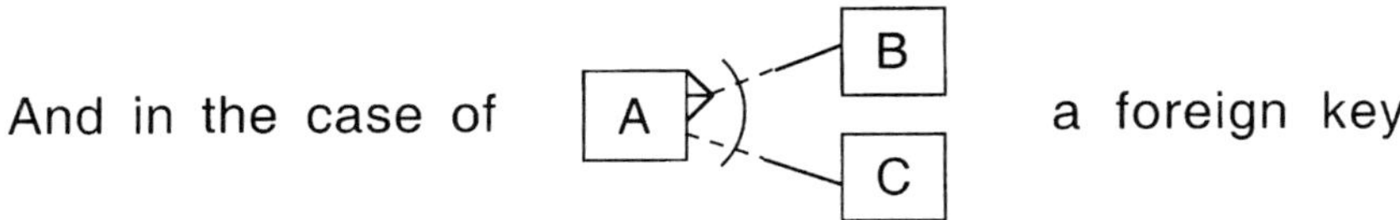

a foreign key field in the 'A' entity table could hold the key to either the 'B' table or the 'C' table or it could be null.

If the B an C keys are not distinct, or not obvious an additional field in the A entity table can be used to indicate whether the foreign key refers to B or C.

5.12 Shared Foreign Key Field Example

In the example:

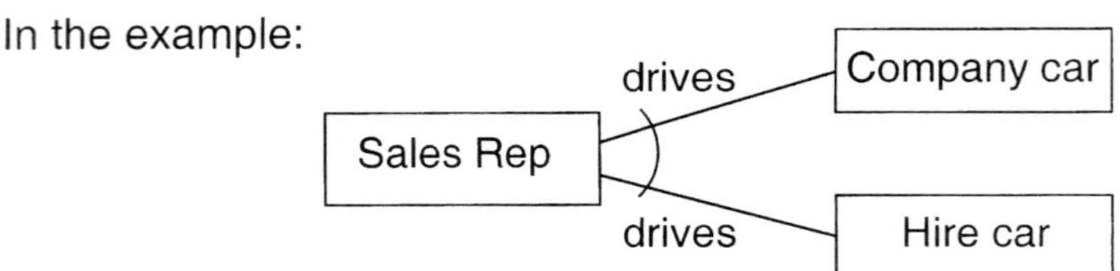

If the entity tables contain:

Sales Rep Table:
Rep.ID -> Name, Sales, Commission

Company Car Table:
Reg.No. -> Make, Model, Miles

Hire Car Table:
Reg.No. -> Hire company, Hire rate

then in this case:

1. The Company Car table and Hire Car table cannot be merged as the data is different.

2. The relationships *could* be modelled by adding the Rep.ID to each car table:

   Reg.No. -> Make, Model, Miles, Rep.ID

   Reg.No. -> Hire company, Hire rate, Rep.ID

3. Better to add the Reg.No. to the Sales Rep table with a field to distinguish the car type:

   Rep.ID ->
   Name, Sales, Commission, Reg.No., Car type

5.13 Single Column Entity Tables

An entity does not need to have any attributes other than the key field or fields.

ie. It is possible for an entity with a single field key to have its key as the only field ....

.... this will give a single column table!

Eg. A theatre seat entity may have only the seat number as a field.

This is perfectly acceptable . . .

But . . . A list of all possible instances of that entity is the *only* information this table provides.

ie. . . . If this information is not required . . .

. . . the entity table can be eliminated.

(though associated relationship tables will still exist)

Eg. A colour entity may exist because an item may have variable numbers of colours . . .

The table may have only one column - the colour.

If it is not necessary to list what colours the item may have, this table can be eliminated.

5.14 Entities Forming a Continuous Sequence

Entity Relationship Modelling assumes:

- entities are not part of any continuous sequence.
- there is, therefore, no ordering or sequence to the rows in the corresponding table.

But sometimes there **is** a significant sequence ....

.... to ignore this is a waste of data storage space.

Eg. Theatre seats may be given different prices depending on where they are in the theatre.

Conventional analysis would give a seat entity with a price attribute:

Seat Row	Seat No.	Price
A	1	£5.00
A	2	£6.00

However, in practice adjacent seats will usually be at the same price which gives the possibility of a more memory efficient table as:

Seat Row	Start No.	Finish No.	Price
A	1	20	£5.00
A	21	40	£6.00

It is possible that this may have been considered from the outset as a "seat block" entity with a price attribute for the seat block .....

.... however this could easily be missed.

5.15 Time Intervals

A common entity sequence is a series of time slots.

Eg. A recreation facility, such as a tennis court, may be bookable in half hour time slots.

Conventional analysis will once again produce a bookings table with a row for each time slot.

No account will be taken of the fact the tennis court is often booked for two or more hours at a time and this will give four or more rows in the bookings table.

Once again it would use less data storage to represent the data with a start time and a finish time.

As with the theatre seat example it is possible to recognise the problem from the outset by creating a time interval entity ....

.... but again this could be easily missed.

This type of storage optimisation is far more easily recognised at the end of the analysis when the tables are derived ....

.... and it only takes a simple adjustment to alter the tables to the optimum format.

It is worth checking to see if a database derived through entity relationship analysis has a table with a sequence of entities that can be optimised in this way.

5.16 Advantages and Disadvantages of Entity Relationship Modelling

Advantages:

The structure given to the data design means that:

1. Data will not be duplicated
2. Data will not be accidentally omitted
3. Empty data fields are avoided
4. It is easy to add new data
5. It is easy to delete old or redundant data
6. It is easy to modify and update existing data
7. It is easy to select and retrieve data for processing

Disadvantages:

None : Entity relationship modelling can only be of assistance to analysis and design.

But : It may not be much use for certain types of system.

ie. It is of little use for systems that are complicated in ways other than data complexity.

5.17 Entity Relationship Modelling : Conclusion

Entity Relationship Modelling provides a systematic approach for handling complicated data systems.

This gives:

1 *An understanding of the system data*

This is useful for detailed requirements analysis.

It may give all the information and understanding required for some types of system.

2. *A overall structure to the data*

This is useful for the overall system design and the detailed design.

This may provide nearly all of the design work required for some types of system.

ie. **Entity Relationship Modelling is useful as both an analysis tool and a design tool.**

CHAPTER 6

Entity Relationship Modelling Case Study

Contents Page

6.1 Entity Relationship Modelling Example

What data tables are needed for a company to keep the following records of personnel and project activities?

For each permanent employee there is a requirement to keep:
- his/her name
- department title and identity code
- the department budget code
- job title
- current projects
- names and dates of training courses attended

The training courses are internal courses set up by each department for their own personnel. Training course details should only be recorded if at least one person has attended.

In addition there are a number of contract workers who need the following information recorded:
- his/her name
- contract hire company name and address
- job title
- current projects

Details of a contact hire company may be kept even if there is currently no contract worker on hire from that company.

There is a requirement to keep, for each project:
- the project budget code
- the start date
- the target completion date

Some larger projects are subdivided into smaller projects which also must be recorded.

A person may work on more than one project at one time. The number of hours worked on each project needs to be recorded for accounting purposes.

It would be useful to record details of a project before anybody participates in it.

6.2 Identifying Entities and Attributes

Possible entities:

Employee, Department, Training Course, Contractor, Contract Company, Project, Hours

Attributes for the suggested entities:

Employee:	Name Job Title
Department:	Department Code Department Name Department Budget Code
Training Course:	Course Title Course Date
Contractor:	Name Job Title
Contract Company:	Contract Company Name
Project:	Project Name Project Budget Code Start Date Target Date
Hours:	Date ??? Start Time ??? Finish Time ???

Note 1: Many of these entities are also likely to need ID numbers for convenient handling.

Note 2: The "Hours" entity seems a little odd but the analysis should clarify this later.

6.3 Identifying the Relationships

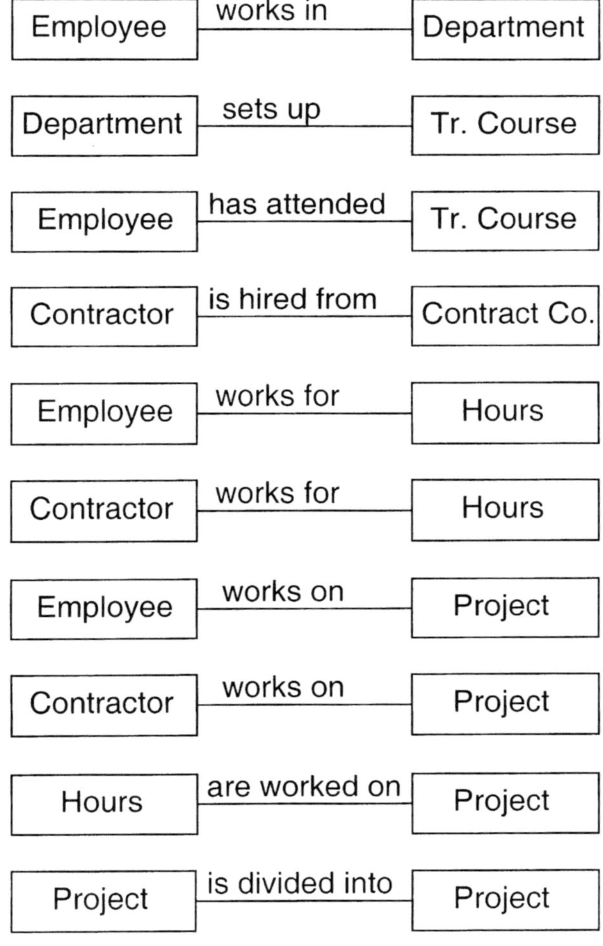

6.4 Considering the Attributes of the Entities

Two entity attributes are fairly long text fields that could be repeated for different entity instances.

An employee or a contractor has a job title:
eg. "Software Engineering Manager"

A training course will have a course title:
eg. "Using the Personnel Database"

For the purposes of this exercise we shall assume:

1. The same job title can occur many times.
2. Information will be required regarding people of the same job title.
   eg. How many Software Engineers worked on project X?
3. Course titles change too frequently so there will be few repeats.
4. With few repeats of course title no information based on course title will be practical.

Either (1) or (2) would be enough to suggest that job title is a separate entity:

eg. 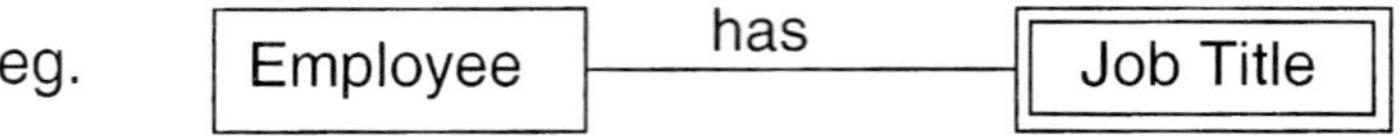

Assumptions (3) and (4) suggest course title should remain as an attribute.

6.5 Considering the Merger of Entities

The Employee and Contractor entities are similar.

They both have attributes: ID Number, Name

Both have relationships:
works for Hours
works on Project
has Job Title

The Employee has the additional relationships:
works in Department
has attended Training Course

The Contractor has the additional relationship:
is hired from Contract Company

Assuming the database will be frequently used to look at data on a project basis from both the employee and contractor tables ....

.... the entity tables *should be merged* into one, "Person" table by:

1. Making the ID Numbers distinctive
   eg. ID numbers for Contractors > 10000

2. Making the Department and Contract Company either-or relationships.

3. Making the Training Course relationship optional (though it was never obligatory for the employee entity anyway!)

6.6 Updating The Relationship List

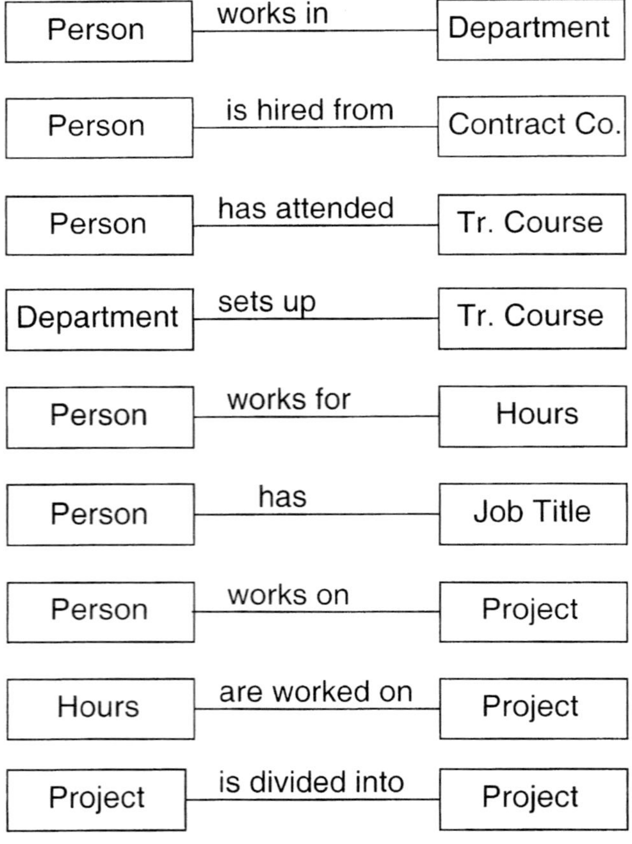

6.7 Categorising The Relationships

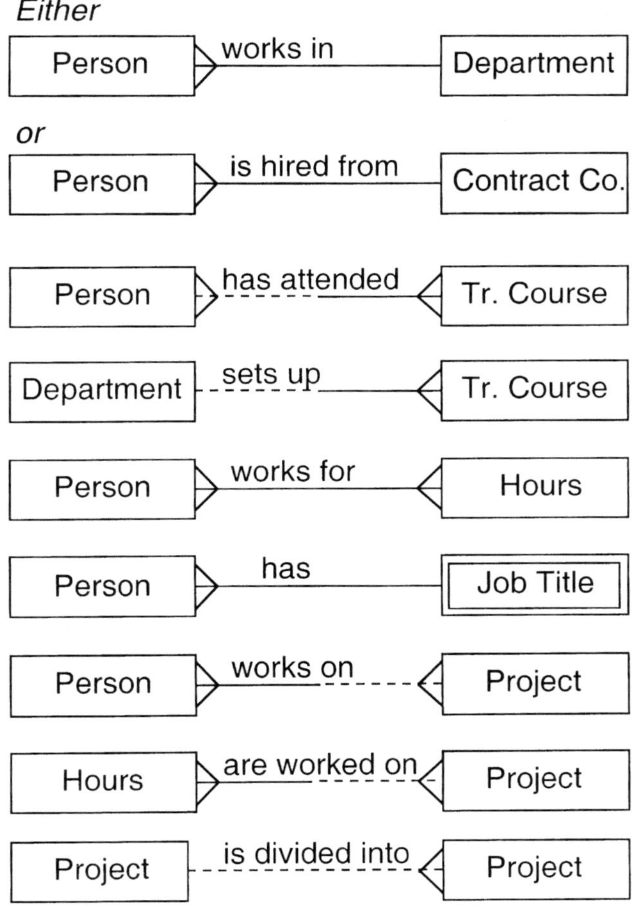

The relationships "Person *works in* Department" and "Person *is hired from* Contract Company" are shown as obligatory for the Person entity as the person **must** belong to either one or the other relationship.

6.8 The Full Entity Relationship Diagram

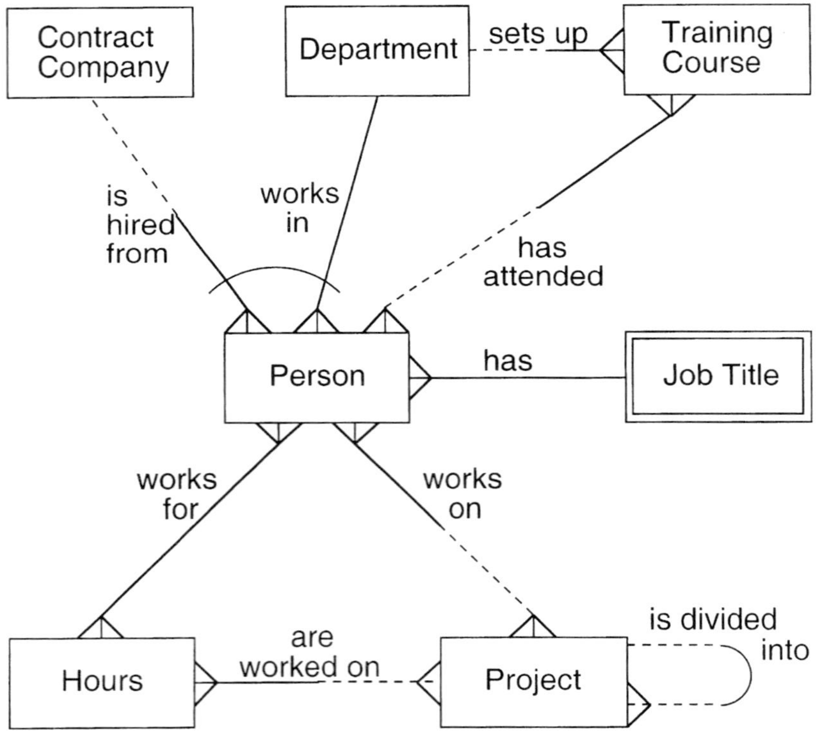

Note that the Contract Co. entity is not a dependant entity despite only having a relationship with one other entity, Person ....

.... This is because a Contract Co. can exist in the database without having any contract worker currently being hired from the company.

6.9 Looking for Redundant Relationships

In the Person/Department/Training Course cycle:

We know .....

(1) who is in each department

(2) at least one department member must have attended any course set up by the department

So we can deduce which courses a department has set up

ie. The relationship "Department sets up Training Course" is redundant

Noting that .....

(1) Department is related to Person only

(2) A department without anyone in it doesn't exist

ie. Department is dependent on the Person entity

(1) Training Course is related to Person only

(2) It is only necessary to keep a record of a Training Course if a person has attended

ie. Training Course is dependent on the Person entity

In the Person/Project/Hours cycle:

No redundancies possible because of the "Fan Trap".

6.10 Looking for 3-Way Relationships

For the Person/Project/Hours relationship cycle:

If we need to know which individual hours (eg. 2pm to 5pm Tuesday of a particular week), are worked on each project by each person ....

then .... we need a three way relationship.

but .... it is only the *total* hours that is needed for each person on each project.

*This tells us a 3-way relationship is **not** required.*

However, it brings into question the "Hours" entity ...

.... do we really need it in this form at all?

The next step may help sort out this rather odd entity.

6.11 Looking for Hidden Entities

Checking all remaining Many to Many relationships:

1. The Person - Training Course relationship has a potential discovered entity called, say, a "Training Course Place".

   But there are

   (1) no useful attributes of this entity,

   (2) no other relationships to this entity,

   so there is no advantage in discovering this entity.

2. The Person - Project relationship has a potential discovered entity called a "Project Role".

   Looking for attributes for Project Role ....

   .... the total hours spent on a project role is necessary for accounting purposes.

   Looking for relationships with Project Role ....

   .... there is obviously a relationship with the Hours entity but the new total hours attribute records all that is needed ....

   .... so we can get rid of the awkward "Hours" entity altogether!

6.12 The Final Entity Relationship Diagram

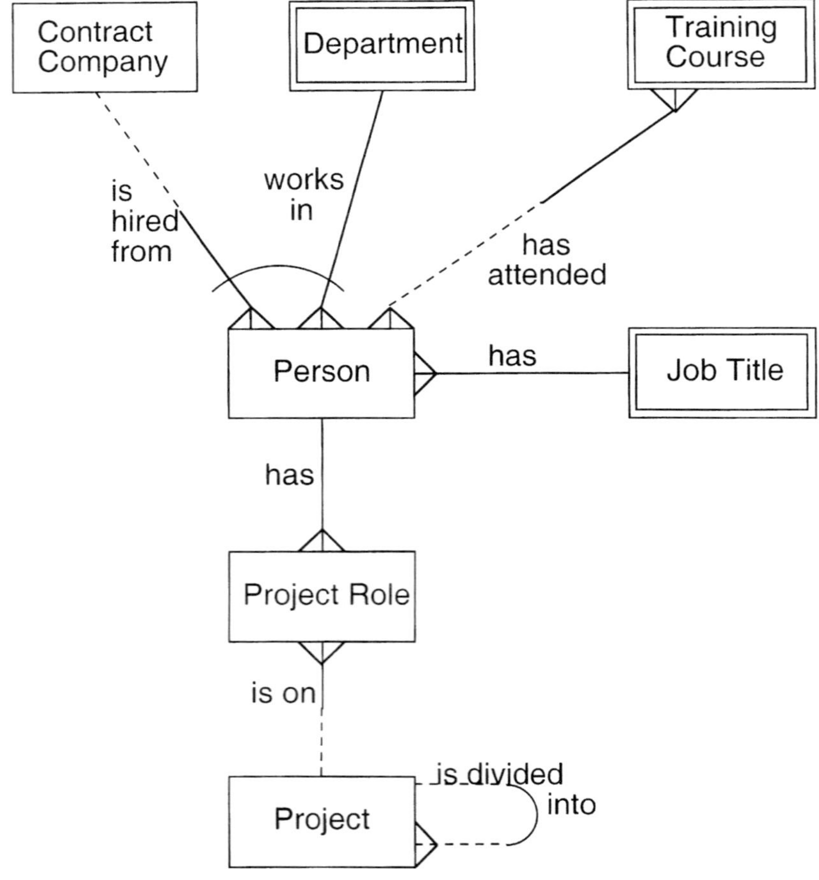

Note that the Department and Training Course are now dependant entities as they have a relationship with only one other entity, Person ....

.... Unlike a Contract Company, a Department or Training Course would not be needed in the database if there were no corresponding Person entity.

6.13 Final Solution: The Entity Data Tables

Putting the "1" entity key fields into the "N" entity tables to represent 1 to N relationships gives:

Person Table:
Person ID -> Person Name, Job ID, Employee Type, Organisation Code

Department Table:
Department Code -> Department Name, Department Budget Code

Contract Company Table:
Contract Company Code -> Contract Company Name

Job Table:
Job ID -> Job Title

Training Course Table:
Course ID -> Course Title, Course Date

Project Role Table:
Person ID, Project ID -> Total Hours Worked

Project Table:
Project ID -> Project Name, Budget Code, Start Date, Target Date

Note: The Employee Type could be a boolean field if such a field type was available. Alternatively it could be a "C" for a contractor or an "E" for an employee.

The Organisation Code would correspond to either a Department Code or a Contract Company Code.

6.14 Final Solution: The Relationship Tables

The N to N relationship for Training Courses gives:

Training Course Attendance Table:
Person ID, Course ID

The Project - *is divided into* - Project relationship is 1 to N but it is optional for the "N" entity.

This means, strictly speaking, a table should be created to represent the relationship of the form:

Project Sub-Division Table:
Master Project ID, Sub Project ID

An alternative solution

If most projects are in fact sub projects of master projects

then this relationship could be represented by extending the project table as in:

Project Table:
Project ID -> Project Name, Budget Code,
Start Date, Target Date,
Master Project ID

But it will mean some rows of the project table will have null entities for the Master Project ID field.

(This will be the only possible null field in the data.)

CHAPTER 7

Basic Data Normalisation

Contents Page

7.1 Data Normalisation

Using Entity-Relationship Analysis the aim is to create a well structured set of data tables without any unnecessary duplication of data.

But....

What check do we have that the optimum data structure has been achieved?

And....

What if we do not have a clean sheet start for the data structure design - suppose a set of tables already exist, how can we improve on the structure?

To achieve these aims a technique was invented by E.J.(Ted) Codd in 1974 known as

"Normalisation"

7.2 Levels of Normalisation

3 levels of normalisation were originally suggested but following input from others this has now been extended to 5.

These levels are known as the first through to the fifth normal forms, (1NF, 2NF, ... 5NF) each higher level being an improvement over lower levels.

A refinement of the third normal form also exists known as the Boyce-Codd normal form (BCNF).

An even higher level known as the domain-key normal form has also been suggested....

.... but this is rather obscure and is really only of theoretical interest.

The advantage of normalisation is that putting tables into ever higher normal forms:

1. Removes and duplication of data

2. Makes the tables easier to change and maintain

ie. *It can make a good data structure out of a bad one!*

7.3 First Normal Form

A table that is not in first normal form is easy to detect....

..... to be in first normal form a table cannot have more than one entry in any field.

Eg. A table not in first normal form:

Table of sales representatives showing each persons sales speciality and the office they use as a base:

First Name	Second Name	Sales Speciality	Base Office
Alice	Alty	computers,printers,netware	London N.
Bert	Brown	software	Sheffield
Cecil	Clarke	computers,printers,software	London N.
Doris	Davis	software,netware	Bristol

The problem:

Most database management systems cannot handle tables that are not in first normal form unless implemented using:

either (1) a long text field.

or (2) a field repeated several times.

7.4 Problems With Tables Not In First Normal Form

In the example Sales Rep table:

The problems with using a long text field for the sales speciality are:

- Searching for a particular sales speciality requires searching for sub strings in the text field....
  .... this is slow if it is possible at all.
- Inserting, modifying or deleting sales specialities will be difficult, slow and error prone.
- There could be wasted space with many partially filled text fields.

The problems with using a field repeated several times with, say, three sales speciality fields are:

- Three separate fields need to be searched when trying to find a particular speciality.
- Inserting, modifying or deleting sales specialities will be difficult, slow and error prone.
- There will be wasted space with null fields.
- If a fourth speciality was acquired by any Sales Rep the method could not handle it at all.

7.5 Putting a Table into First Normal Form

To put a table into first normal form, duplicate the rest of the row for each entry in the offending field:

So the table:

First Name	Second Name	Sales Speciality	Base Office
Alice	Alty	computers,printers,netware	London N.
Bert	Brown	software	Sheffield
Cecil	Clarke	computers,printers,software	London N.
Doris	Davis	software,netware	Bristol

becomes:

First Name	Second Name	Sales Speciality	Base Office
Alice	Alty	computers	London N.
Alice	Alty	printers	London N.
Alice	Alty	netware	London N.
Bert	Brown	software	Sheffield
Cecil	Clarke	computers	London N.
Cecil	Clarke	printers	London N.
Cecil	Clarke	software	London N.
Doris	Davis	software	Bristol
Doris	Davis	netware	Bristol

Clearly there is much duplication in the new format, but this is taken care of when putting the table into higher normal forms.

7.6 Keys Fields

To consider higher normal forms the concept of a key must be clear.

If a field is different for every row of a table then it can be used to identify each row and hence it is called a *key* field.

Alternatively, there may not be any one field that is unique for all rows - a combination of columns may be required for a key.

Eg. The key for the sales team table is a combination of the rows First name, Second name, and Sales speciality.

N.B. A key field or combination of fields must be unique for *all possible* rows as well as existing rows.

For the sales team it is assumed that no two people will have the whole name the same....

.... but it may be possible for two people to have either a common first name or a common second name....

.... therefore both names must be included in the key.

Note: The assumption that each whole name is unique is dangerous - this is why people are frequently referred to by an ID number of some sort.

7.7 Dependant Fields

The concept of dependant fields is also needed for consideration of higher normal forms.

If we know what the value in a particular field will be once we know the values in some other fields, we can say that field is dependant on those other fields.

Eg. Once we know the complete sales rep name we know what the base office will be.

ie. The base office is *dependant* on the first and second names.

However, we don't know the sales speciality for a given sales rep's name as there may be several possibilities.

ie. The sales speciality is *not dependant* on the sales rep's name.

All fields will be dependant on the key fields in a table.

If a field or set of fields determines another then these are said to be *determinant* fields.

Eg. The base office depends on the first and second names, therefore the first and second names are the determinants of the base field.

7.8 Second Normal Form

For a table to be in the second normal form all non key fields must depend on the whole table key.

ie. If a table is in first normal form it can only fail to be in second normal form if it has more than one field for the key.

Eg. The sales team table is not in second normal form because:

(1) The key consists of the first name, second name and sales speciality fields.

(2) The base office is dependant on only part of that key, the first name and second name.

7.9 Problems of Tables Not in Second Normal Form

(1) Information is duplicated.

eg. The data that Alice Alty is based in North London exists in three separate rows.

This is a waste of storage space

(2) Data entry is laborious and more error prone as unnecessary extra input is required

(3) Altering the data is difficult as it will need to be altered in more than one place

Eg. If Alice Alty moved to the Bristol office

(4) There is a possibility of anomalies in the data through errors of input or incomplete alteration such that the data becomes inconsistent.

(5) Null fields are more likely to be required.

Eg. If a new sales rep is entered before he has any sales speciality a row must be created with a null speciality field.

(6) Information is more easily lost when data is deleted.

Eg. If the sales company stops dealing in software and all rows containing this data are deleted, then the name Bert Brown and information giving his base office is lost.

7.10 Putting Tables into Second Normal Form

Two (or more) tables must be created to replace the original to put the table in second normal form.

Each field that depends on less than the whole key must be removed and put into a new table:

Table 1:

First Name	Second Name	Sales Speciality
Alice	Alty	computers
Alice	Alty	printers
Alice	Alty	netware
Bert	Brown	software
Cecil	Clarke	computers
Cecil	Clarke	printers
Cecil	Clarke	software
Doris	Davis	software
Doris	Davis	netware

Table 2:

First Name	Second Name	Base Office
Alice	Alty	London N.
Bert	Brown	Sheffield
Cecil	Clarke	London N.
Doris	Davis	Bristol

Any new personal information such as their telephone number can now be added to Table 2 without any repetition.

It is also more obvious that any information which is related to both name and sales speciality, such as the total value of sales must be added to Table 1.

7.11 Third Normal Form

Consider the following table in second normal form:

First Name	Second Name	Base Office	Telephone Number	Extension Number
Alice	Alty	London N.	0181-2345678	246
Bert	Brown	Sheffield	0114-2555666	421
Cecil	Clarke	London N.	0181-2345678	255
Doris	Davis	Bristol	0117-9444333	246
Eric	Evans	London E.	0181-2345678	322

The key is the combination of first and second name.

Note that all field entries depend on the whole key....

.... but notice the telephone number is also dependant on the base office (though not vice-versa).

ie. The information giving the telephone number of each office is repeated for as many times as there are sales reps based at that office.

This duplication of data will give all the associated problems of tables not in second normal form.

The table needs to be put in <u>third normal form</u> which requires the table to be in second normal form and to have all non key fields dependant *only* on the key.

ie. To be in third normal form each field must depend on the key, the whole key, and nothing but the key!

7.12 Putting Tables into Third Normal Form

To put a table into third normal form the action is similar to putting a table into second normal form.

ie. Put the dependant field into a separate table with its determinant field(s) as the key.

So the table is split into two tables as follows:

Table 1:

First Name	Second Name	Base Office	Extension Number
Alice	Alty	London N.	246
Bert	Brown	Sheffield	221
Cecil	Clarke	London N.	255
Doris	Davis	Bristol	246
Eric	Evans	London E.	322

Table 2:

Base Office	Telephone Number
London N.	0181-2345678
Sheffield	0114-2555666
Bristol	0117-9444333
London E.	0181-2345678

(Note: Thanks to the wonders of modern telephony it is quite possible for two sites that are reasonably close to share a common telephone number.)

The saving in this particular table is very small as we have only a small sample of sales reps....

.... if there had been many sales reps at each office the saving could have been considerable.

CHAPTER 8

Advanced Data Normalisation

Contents Page

8.1 Duplication of Data in Third Normal Form

The trouble with using a name as a key is that a name such as John Smith is often not unique.

Suppose that the sales company required each sales rep's telephone number and extension to be entered as a unique identifier in all administrative procedures.

A look-up table to be able to find out the rep's name and base office may then be required:

Telephone Number	Extension Number	First Name	Second Name	Base Office
0181-2345678	246	Alice	Alty	London N.
0114-2555666	421	Bert	Brown	Sheffield
0181-2345678	255	Cecil	Clarke	London N.
0117-9444333	246	Doris	Davis	Bristol
0181-2345678	322	Eric	Evans	London E.
0117-9444333	234	Bert	Brown	Bristol

With the telephone and extension numbers as the key fields *this table is already in third normal form!*

ie. Each non key field is dependant on the whole key

\+ No non key field is dependant on any other non key field

But once again ....

The information giving the telephone number of each office is repeated for as many times as there are sales reps based at that office!

8.2 Third Normal Form Inconsistency

An alternative key exists for the given table.

Instead of: Telephone number + Extension Number

the key could be: Base office + Extension number

This gives:

Base Office	Extension Number	First Name	Second Name	Telephone Number
London N.	246	Alice	Alty	0181-2345678
Sheffield	421	Bert	Brown	0114-2555666
London N.	255	Cecil	Clarke	0181-2345678
Bristol	246	Doris	Davis	0117-9444333
London E.	322	Eric	Evans	0181-2345678
Bristol	234	Bert	Brown	0117-9444333

Looked at in this form the table fails to meet the requirements for second normal form ....

.... as the telephone number is based only on part of the key, the Base office.

ie. As before, the table must be split to remove the telephone number field and place it in a new table with the base office as its key.

This inconsistency in the third normal form can only occur if:

(1) There is more than one possible key

(2) Each key is a multiple field key

(3) The possible key's each share a common field.

8.3 The Boyce-Codd Normal Form

The possible inconsistency in the third normal form was pointed out by Raymond Boyce shortly after Codd invented the first three normal forms.

Codd then refined the third normal form to specify that the rules for the third normal form should apply *regardless of which key is chosen.*

This new form is referred to as the Boyce-Codd normal form to distinguish it from the original third normal form.

Another way of specifying the Boyce-Codd normal form is:

> *If a field is dependant on one or more other fields then those other fields must be a possible key for the table.*

The problem with tables not in Boyce-Codd normal form:

> Such tables still have duplication of information with all the associated problems this brings.

The remedy:

> Split the table with the same technique as putting a table into the second or third normal form.

8.4 Joining Tables Together

Splitting tables into smaller tables may be a good idea to reduce duplication of information ....

.... but what if we wanted the information in it's non normalised form?

eg. The telephone extension look-up table with:

Telephone no. + extension + names + base office

has been split into:

(1) base office + extension + names

(2) base office + telephone number

But ....

The sales company still needs to find out the name of a sales rep and their base office given their telephone number and extension.

Most database management systems provide some means of joining tables back together for displaying information or generating printed reports.

ie. *It is still possible to print out the following even though the data has been normalised into two tables:*

Telephone Number	Extension Number	First Name	Second Name	Base Office
0181-2345678	246	Alice	Alty	London N.
0114-2555666	421	Bert	Brown	Sheffield

etc...

8.5 Methods of Joining Tables Together

In the example, if the two tables were known as `Name` and `Tel` the standard SQL database query language command for displaying the original table could be:

```
SELECT  Tel.TelNum, Name.ExtNum,
        Name.FirstName, Name.SecondName,
        Name.BaseOffice
  FROM  Name, Tel
 WHERE  Name.BaseOffice = Tel.BaseOffice;
```

The `WHERE` part of this command informs the database management system how to join the two tables at the time they are displayed.

Database management systems that do not use SQL commands may require the join condition to be specified before the display command is given.

In either case the lines of output are worked out when the display is generated ....

.... the joined table is not actually created and stored anywhere.

Many systems allow the join mechanism to be permanently set up by creating a virtual table of the joined tables known as a "view".

Although it can be examined like a real table, in reality a view selects the information from the underlying base tables whenever it is used.

8.6 Possibilities of Higher Normal Forms

Suppose the sales reps are allocated to specific customers as well as having their sales speciality.

A table showing who sells what to which customer could be as follows:

First Name	Second Name	Sales Speciality	Customer
Alice	Alty	computers	Hackett Software Co.
Alice	Alty	printers	Hackett Software Co.
Alice	Alty	netware	Hackett Software Co.
Alice	Alty	computers	Pi-Rates Ltd.
Alice	Alty	printers	Pi-Rates Ltd.
Alice	Alty	netware	Pi-Rates Ltd.
Bert	Brown	software	Hackett Software Co.
Bert	Brown	software	Flog-It-Quick Retailers
Bert	Brown	software	C.D.Finance Plc.
Cecil	Clarke	computers	Flog-It-Quick Retailers
Cecil	Clarke	printers	Flog-It-Quick Retailers
Cecil	Clarke	software	Flog-It-Quick Retailers
Cecil	Clarke	computers	Pi-Rates Ltd.
Cecil	Clarke	printers	Pi-Rates Ltd.
Cecil	Clarke	software	Pi-Rates Ltd.

There is no choice of key as all four columns are required for the key, so the table is automatically in Boyce-Codd normal form as well as third normal form.

There appears to be still a lot of duplication....

.... but can this duplication be avoided?

8.7 Multi-Value Dependencies

A multi-value dependency occurs when a field would contain more than one value if we went backwards and took the table out of first normal form.

eg. In our original table of the sales team:

First Name	Second Name	Sales Speciality	Base Office
Alice	Alty	computers,printers,netware	London N.
Bert	Brown	software	Sheffield
Cecil	Clarke	computers,printers,software	London N.
Doris	Davis	software,netware	Bristol

The sales speciality is a multi-valued dependency of the combined first and second names.

Further reduction of duplication of information by putting the table in normal forms higher than the Boyce-Codd normal form is possible....

*.... **if** there is more than one multi-value dependency.*

This in turn can only occur for tables in Boyce-Codd normal form if:

(1) there are at least three columns in the table

and (2) all the fields are required to make up the key

8.8 Example of More Than One Multi-Value Dependency

The table showing who sells what to which customer has two multiple dependencies:

First Name	Second Name	Sales Speciality	Customer
Alice	Alty	computers, printers, netware	Hackett Software Co., Pi-Rates Ltd.
Bert	Brown	software	Hackett Software Co., Flog-It-Quick Retailers, C.D.Finance plc.
Cecil	Clarke	computers, printers, software	Flog-It-Quick Retailers, Pi-Rates Ltd.

These multi-value fields are completely independent of each other.

ie. When the table is put in first normal form there is a row for every possible combination of sales speciality and customer for each sales rep.

This independence means the table needs to be put into *fourth normal form.*

8.9 Putting a Table Into Fourth Normal Form

To put a table into fourth normal form the table needs to be split so that there is no more than one multi-value dependency in each new table.

So the table showing who sells what to which customer becomes:

Table 1:

First Name	Second Name	Sales Speciality
Alice	Alty	computers
Alice	Alty	printers
Alice	Alty	netware
Bert	Brown	software
Cecil	Clarke	computers
Cecil	Clarke	printers
Cecil	Clarke	software

Table 2:

First Name	Second Name	Customer
Alice	Alty	Hackett Software Co.
Alice	Alty	Pi-Rates Ltd.
Bert	Brown	Hackett Software Co.
Bert	Brown	Flog-It-Quick Retailers
Bert	Brown	C.D.Finance Plc.
Cecil	Clarke	Flog-It-Quick Retailers
Cecil	Clarke	Pi-Rates Ltd.

As well as a potential saving of storage space it will be now far easier to add new entries to these tables or to make changes to any speciality or customer.

8.10 Related Multi-Value Dependencies

Suppose a table has more than one multi-value dependency but they are not totally independent of each other:

First Name	Second Name	Sales Speciality	Customer
Alice	Alty	computers	Hackett Software Co.
Alice	Alty	printers	Hackett Software Co.
Alice	Alty	printers	Pi-Rates Ltd.
Alice	Alty	netware	Pi-Rates Ltd.
Bert	Brown	software	Hackett Software Co.
Bert	Brown	software	Flog-It-Quick Retailers
Bert	Brown	software	C.D.Finance Plc.
Cecil	Clarke	computers	Flog-It-Quick Retailers
Cecil	Clarke	printers	Flog-It-Quick Retailers
Cecil	Clarke	software	Flog-It-Quick Retailers
Cecil	Clarke	printers	Pi-Rates Ltd.
Cecil	Clarke	software	Pi-Rates Ltd.

Every combination of sales speciality with customer does not necessarily exist for each sales rep.

ie.
- Alice Alty does not sell netware to Hackett Software.
- Neither Alice Alty or Cecil Clarke sells computers to Pi-Rates Ltd.

Splitting the table into two as described for fourth normal form would loose this information.

8.11 Fifth Normal Form

If:

(1) a table has at least 3 columns

(2) all the fields are required to make up the key

(3) there are two or more multi-valued dependencies

(4) *there is a definable relationship between these multi-valued dependencies*

(5) *this relationship is independent of any other field*

.... then duplication of information can be reduced by putting the table in **fifth normal form**.

In the example given the definable relationship is:

1. Hackett Software does not buy netware from anybody

2. Pi-Rates Ltd. does not buy computers from anybody

3. All other customers will buy any of the products from any sales rep.

This relationship can be expressed in a table defining which customer buys which product specialities.

8.12 Putting a Table Into Fifth Normal Form

To put the table of who sells what to which company into fifth normal form three tables need to be created:

1. The table of who sells what
2. The table of who sells to which customer
3. The table of which customer buys what

The first two of these tables are the same as described for putting into fourth normal form, but now the extra table is necessary.

The relationship between the sales speciality and the customers is difficult to see from the original table.

This means on the original table it would be difficult to add a new sales speciality-customer relationship such as if Flog-It-Quick Retailers decided to buy printers....

.... but with the new table it is simple.

But ....

the difficulty in seeing the relationship also means it can be difficult to detect that the tables need to be put into fifth normal form.

8.13 Example of Tables in Fifth Normal Form

Table 1:

First Name	Second Name	Sales Speciality
Alice	Alty	computers
Alice	Alty	printers
Alice	Alty	netware
Bert	Brown	software
Cecil	Clarke	computers
Cecil	Clarke	printers
Cecil	Clarke	software

Table 2:

First Name	Second Name	Customer
Alice	Alty	Hackett Software Co.
Alice	Alty	Pi-Rates Ltd.
Bert	Brown	Hackett Software Co.
Bert	Brown	Flog-It-Quick Retailers
Bert	Brown	C.D.Finance Plc.
Cecil	Clarke	Flog-It-Quick Retailers
Cecil	Clarke	Pi-Rates Ltd.

Table 3:

Sales Speciality	Customer
computers	Hackett Software Co.
printers	Hackett Software Co.
software	Hackett Software Co.
software	C.D.Finance Plc.
computers	Flog-It-Quick Retailers
printers	Flog-It-Quick Retailers
software	Flog-It-Quick Retailers
printers	Pi-Rates Ltd.
software	Pi-Rates Ltd.
netware	Pi-Rates Ltd.

8.14 Merging Tables

Normalisation tends to fragment larger tables into many smaller tables ....

.... sometimes these smaller tables should then be put together to make larger tables again.

If the tables have the same key fields

and the table entries cover the same domain (ie. each row in one table has a corresponding row in the other)

then the tables can be merged.

Notes:

1. Tables with the same key should only occur if they are derived from different larger tables.

2. If the domains of the two tables are not the same then some null fields will result in any merged table.

3. Strictly speaking different domains mean the tables should not be merged...

   ...but it may still be convenient to do so if they are nearly the same as there will only be a few null entries.

8.15 Example of Merging Tables

Suppose there is a table of sales rep information:

ID No.	First Name	Second Name	Base Office
1010	Alice	Alty	London N.
1623	Bert	Brown	Sheffield
1278	Cecil	Clarke	London N.
etc...			

and also a table of the commission earned:

ID No.	Commission
1010	£2500
1623	£3500
1278	£1750
etc...	

If this second table holds no record for anyone other than Sales Reps

and ***ALL*** Sales Reps earn commission

then these can be combined into:

ID No.	First name	Second name	Base office	Commission
1010	Alice	Alty	London N.	£2500
1623	Bert	Brown	Sheffield	£3500
1278	Cecil	Clarke	London N.	£1750
etc...				

8.16 A Final Check

Having put all tables into 5th Normal Form, including any merged tables, the normalisation process is complete ....

.... however, it is always worth making a common sense check that the data tables are in their optimum format:

- Are there any tables containing separate rows for a sequence of entities or time slots? If so, could this be better represented by columns for the start and finish of a range? (See sections 5.14 and 5.15)

  Normalisation will not produce this optimisation.

- Are there any totals or other calculated fields stored? Eg. A parent table could have the number of children as an attribute, with the children listed separately in another table.

  This is a form of duplication of data which is unlikely to be detected through normalisation.

- Can any data be derived from data elsewhere? Eg. A table may show which supervisors are on duty on each day of the week, but elsewhere there may be a table specifying which days of the week a supervisor is not working.

  This is another form of duplication which is unlikely to be detected through normalisation.

This final, common sense check is the last step in the design of the data table structure by normalisation.

CHAPTER 9

Normalisation and Entity Relationship Modelling

Contents Page

9.1 Objectives Compared

The objectives of E-R Modelling are:

1. To help develop an understanding of the nature of the data complexities in the system.

2. To be able to organise the data into a logical, "structured" form with each data item where it may be expected (useful for maintenance).

3. To be able to organise the data in an efficient way so that data is neither duplicated or omitted.

The end result is (hopefully) the "system data dictionary" which defines:

1. The data tables that appear in the system.

2. The fields (ie. columns) for each entry in the table.

3. A key for each table, consisting of one or more of these fields.

This is similar to the Normalisation objectives so how are Normalisation and E-R Modelling related?

9.2 Identifying the Entities and Attributes

The first step was to identify the entities and the attributes for those entities.

It may not be clear whether an item is an entity or an attribute so the following hints were made:

E-R Hint : Variable Numbers of an Attribute

Check the attributes of all entities -

Are there variable numbers of an attribute?

Eg. An item may have several different colours.

If so then make the attribute a separate entity or there will be blank fields in the data base ....

..... this can give unexpected entities such as Colour.

ie. If an item can have several colours,

and different items have different numbers of colours

then the colour must be a separate entity.

but If all the items had multiple colours but each had the same number of colours there would be no need of a separate colour entity.

This process is exactly the same as the first step of normalisation .....

ie. it is putting the entity table into 1st normal form

E-R Hint : Attributes With Attributes

Check the attributes of all entities -

Has any attribute got an attribute of its own?

Eg. A person entity may have a car type and a car length as attributes . . .

. . . in this case the car length is really an attribute of the car type.

If an attribute has an attribute of its own then it should be made into a separate entity....

.... otherwise the attributes are interdependent and there is a risk that the data base could become inconsistent.

Eg. A persons car type may be changed with the user forgetting to change the car length . . .

. . . this could lead to two people with the same car type but with different car lengths.

This process is exactly the same as the third step of normalisation .....

ie. it is putting the entity table into 3rd normal form, or 2nd normal form if an attribute depends on an "attribute" that is really part of the key.

E-R Hint : Repeated, Long Text Attributes

Check the attributes of all entities -

Is any long text attribute likely to be repeated for different occurrences of the entity?

eg. More than one person may have the same car type, such as "Ford Escort Estate".

ie. If there are many repeats

or the text is long

then there can be a significant space saving by making this attribute into a separate entity referenced by an ID number.

ie. A separate table should be created with the text and an associated identity number . . .

. . . other tables will then refer to the ID number rather than the text itself.

This process is also the same as the third step of normalisation .....

ie. Once an ID number has been created the text field is dependent on that number, so this process is putting the entity table back into 3rd normal form.

E-R Hint : Text Attributes Used In Matchings

Check the attributes of all entities -

> *Is any text attribute likely to be tested for matching entries?*

Even if the text is short with only a few repeats . . .

if   tests may be made for matching entries,

then   it should be a separate entity.

Eg. A `TOWN` attribute could have any of the entries:

```
Leicester Leics  Leic   Leics. Leic.
LEICESTER LEICS  LEIC   LEICS. LEIC.
```

This is OK if it is only used as part of an address. . .

But .... if matching on the name is to be done, (eg. to list all people from Leicester)

then entries may be missed!

So .... If the field is made a separate entity then each name would be stored once only with only one representation.

Once again process is the same as the third step of normalisation .....

ie. Once an ID number has been created the text field is dependent on that number, so this process is putting the entity table back into 3rd normal form.

9.3 Where Do Multiple Field Keys come From?

1. Entities where the entity identifier requires two or more fields:

   eg. First name and second name

   Date and time

   Telephone number and extension

2. Relationships between entities.

   Relationships that are classified as:

   N to N (many to many)

   1 to N which is optional for the 'N' entity

   1 to 1 which is optional for both entities

   All (in theory) produce a separate relation table with the key being a combination of the key fields from the two entity tables.

   (In practice a separate relation table is not required for the 1 to N or 1 to 1 relationships if blank fields are allowed in the entity tables).

3. Discovered Entity Tables

   These are similar to relationship tables except there may be further, non key fields for:

   (1) additional attributes.

   (2) additional 1 to 1 or N to 1 relationships that can be modelled by adding the other entity key as a field in the discovered entity table.

9.4 E-R Modelling and the 2nd, 3rd and Boyce-Codd Normal Forms

Data tables derived from entity relationship modelling should automatically be in 2nd Normal Form because:

- for entity tables with multiple field keys correct choice of entities and attributes should put the entity table in both 2nd and 3rd normal form.

- for relationship tables there are no non key fields.

- for discovered entities any attributes of the discovered entity must depend on the whole key....

  .... otherwise they will depend on the key for one of the original entities it is discovered between.

  ie. They should be in a different entity's table.

The 1st and 3rd normal form will also be satisfied by correctly choosing the entities and attributes ....

.... as will the Boyce-Codd normal form if enough care is taken over attribute dependencies ....

.... so a good E-R analysis will automatically give tables in Boyce-Codd Normal Form.

9.5 Tables With 3 or More Fields in Their Keys

Tables normalised to 3rd/Boyce-Codd normal form will not require further normalisation unless:

1. There are at least 3 fields in the key.
2. There are no non key fields.

This will only occur if:

1. A single entity needs three fields for the key

   Eg. Day + Month + Year
   Exchange no. + telephone no. + extension

   These tables will normally be in 5th normal form.

2. A relationship table relates two entities, one of which has a two field key.

   These tables will normally be in 5th normal form.

3. A relationship table relates 3 different entities.

   These tables may require further normalisation.

4. An entity is discovered between two other entities, one of which has a two field key.

   These tables will normally be in 5th normal form.

5. An entity is discovered between 3 other entities.

   If there are no other attributes or relationships these tables resemble three way relationship tables *and may require further normalisation.*

9.6 Three Way Relationship Tables

3-way relationships are created when it is found that other links do not supply all the desired information:

ie.

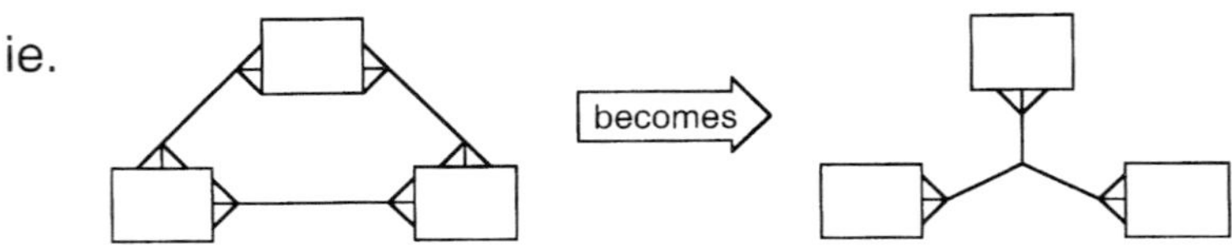

Alternatively an entity can be "discovered" between two entities which then leads to relationships being remodelled to link to the new entity:

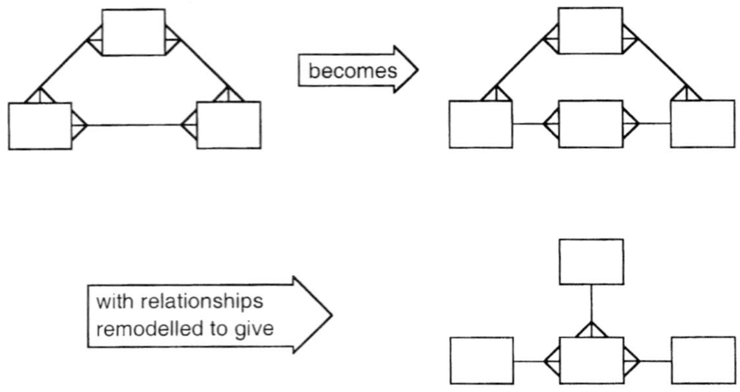

It is also possible to derive the 3-way discovered entity directly, but this is less intuitive.

However, if no further attributes or relationships are found for the new entity it will give the same table as the 3-way relationship.

9.7 Normalisation of 3-Way Relationship Tables

Normalisation to 4th or 5th normal forms has the opposite effect of creating a three way relationship.

ie. The single 3-way relationship table is broken down into 2-way relationship tables.

Normalising to 4th normal form is equivalent to converting:

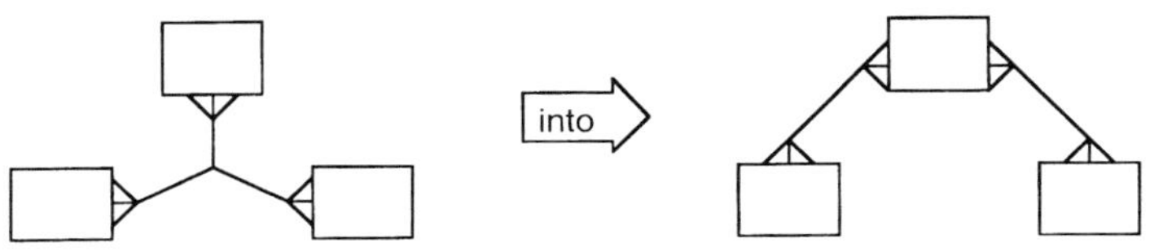

.... which then results in two relationship tables.

Normalising to 5th normal form is equivalent to converting:

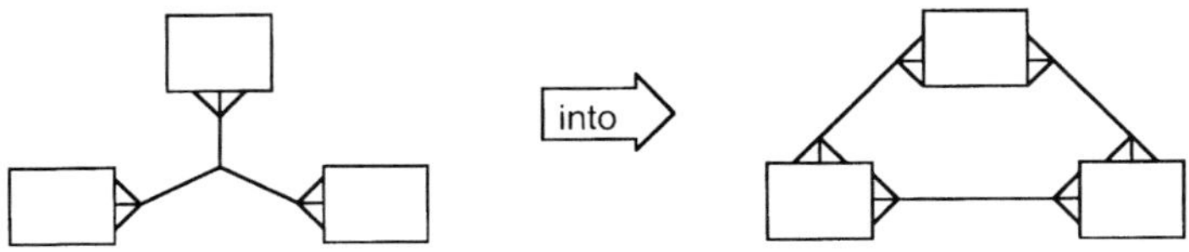

.... which then results in three relationship tables.

If either of the above is possible it shows the original creation of the 3-way relationship was a mistake!

9.8 Advantages of Entity Relationship Analysis and Normalisation Used Together

Entity Relationship Analysis has the advantages:

1 It gives a means of starting a data structure design from scratch.

2. It is diagrammatic - this makes it easier to understand which in turn:

   (1) helps to clarify the mind of the user

   (2) helps to communicate the ideas to others for checking

Normalisation helps to:

1. Check the database structure design is correct

2. Correct any database structure design faults

3. Clarify difficult areas of E-R data structure design such as 3-way relationship tables.

Together they give a data table structure where:

1. Data will not be duplicated or omitted.

2. Empty data fields are avoided.

3. It is easy to view, add, delete, or update data.

CHAPTER 10

Data Normalisation Case Study

Contents Page

10.1 Normalisation Example: A Bus Company

A bus company has a large fleet of busses which it runs over an extensive network of bus routes. It believes it gives a high level of service to its customers and it also takes pride in the training it gives its many drivers.

Each driver must have received a training session on each make and model of bus before he or she is allowed to drive that bus type. In addition, no driver can drive any particular route without being trained for that route.

In the interests of service a log is kept of which driver and which bus is used for every bus run so that any complaints can be traced to the person and vehicle responsible. A driver is only ever assigned to one route and one bus in a day, though the bus may be re-used on another route on a different shift.

Each bus is kept in good working order with a record being kept of when it was last serviced and how often a bus of that make and model requires a service. Most busses can be used on most routes but there are some restrictions about where the larger busses may go, and the smaller ones are not used on high demand routes.

The bus company's records are kept on computer using a modern database management system with the information organised and stored in four tables.

How can the data structure be improved?

10.2 The Bus Company Tables

1. The Driver Table

This gives data about each driver in the following fields:

Driver ID : A unique number for each driver

Title : Mr./Mrs./Miss

Name : Driver's name

Training : The bus types (ie. makes and models) of each bus he/she is trained to drive

D.O.B. : Date of birth

Grade : The driver's job grade

Salary : The salary for drivers at this grade

2. The Permission Table

This records all possible combinations of which driver is allowed to take which type of bus on which route, and has the following fields:

Driver ID : The unique ID number for each driver.

Route : The route identification number

Bus Type : The bus make and model

Capacity : The number of passengers a bus of this type can carry

3. The Log Table

Records for each bus trip (specified by the day, time and route) the bus number, the driver and other associated information in the following fields:

Day : The date

Time : The time of the start of a bus trip

Route : The route identification number

Direction: Bus direction= "outward" or "inward"

Driver ID : The unique ID number for each driver

Bus Reg : The registration number of the bus

Bus Type : The bus make and model

Freq. : The number of busses per day on the route

Duration : The average length of time that a bus on this route is expected to take

4. The Service Table

Records details of the busses servicing in the following fields:

Bus Reg : The registration number of the bus

Last Serv : The date of the last service

Interval : The prescribed number of months between services for this type of bus

10.3 Restructuring The Driver Table into First and Second Normal Form

First Normal Form

This table is not even in first normal form.

The *Training* field contains multiple entries of the type referred to in other tables as *Bus Type*.

Each row should be repeated for as many entries there are in the *Training* field so there is only one entry in this field in each row.

The *Training* field can then be renamed *Bus Type* to be consistent with the other tables.

Second Normal Form

The new key for the table is *Driver ID + Bus Type*. All other fields are dependent on the *Driver ID* only.

To put into second normal form the table should then be split into:

1. A **Bus Training Table** with fields:

   Driver ID + Bus Type

   This table cannot be further normalised.

2. A new **Driver Table** with fields:

   Driver ID -> Title, Name, D.O.B., Grade, Salary

Notation = *key field + key field +... -> non key field, non key field...*

10.4 Restructuring The Driver Table into Third and Final Normal Form

Third Normal Form

In the modified **Driver Table** the *Salary* is dependant on the *Grade*. This should be split from the rest of the table to give:

1. A **Salary Table** with fields:

   Grade -> Salary

   This table cannot be further normalised.

2. A new **Driver Table** with fields:

   Driver ID -> Title, Name, D.O.B., Grade

   This table cannot be further normalised.

Result

The original Driver Table becomes:

1. **Bus Training Table** : *Driver ID + Bus Type*

2. **Salary Table** : *Grade -> Salary*

3. **Driver Table** :
   Driver ID -> Title, Name, D.O.B., Grade

Notation = *key field + key field +... -> non key field, non key field...*

10.5 Restructuring The Permission Table into First, Second and Third Normal Form

First Normal Form

The table is already in first normal form

Second Normal Form

The key to this table is *Driver ID + Route + Bus Type.*

However, Capacity depends only on Bus Type.

The table should therefore be split to give:

1. A new **Permission Table** with fields:

   Driver ID + Route + Bus Type

2. A **Bus Type Table** with fields:

   Bus Type -> Capacity

   This table cannot be further normalised.

Third Normal Form, Boyce-Codd Normal Form

The Permission Table is already in third normal form and Boyce-Codd normal form.

10.6 Restructuring The Permission Table into Fourth and Fifth Normal Form

Fourth Normal Form

There is two multi-value dependencies in the Permission table:

1. the routes a driver is trained to drive
2. the bus types the driver is trained to drive.

The two multi-value dependencies are not totally independent of each other, however, as not all bus types are used on all routes.

The table, therefore, already counts as being in fourth normal form.

Fifth Normal Form

A relationship between the multi-valued dependencies of the Permission Table can be simply established by introducing a table showing what bus types are used on each route.

Thus the Permission table becomes:

1. A **Bus Training Table** with fields:
   Driver ID + Bus Type

2. A **Route Training Table** with fields:
   Driver ID + Route

3. A **Bus Use Table** with fields:
   Bus Type + Route

10.7 Results From The Driver and Permission Tables

The Bus Training Table has been derived from both the original Driver Table and Original Permission Table....

These tables should correspond, if not, a data entry error has occurred!

Therefore, the resulting tables so far are:

1. **Bus Training Table** : *Driver ID + Bus Type*
2. **Salary Table** : *Grade -> Salary*
3. **Driver Table** :
   Driver ID -> Title, Name, D.O.B., Grade
4. **Bus Type Table** : *Bus Type -> Capacity*
5. **Route Training Table** : *Driver ID + Route*
6. **Bus Use Table** : *Bus Type + Route*

10.8 Restructuring The Log Table Into First, Second and Third Normal Forms

The table is already in first normal form.

The key to the table is *Day+Time+Route+Direction*, but *Freq.* and *Duration* are only dependant on the *Route* field.

ie. To put into second normal form these fields should be split from the Log Table into a table with route information.

This still leaves the Log Table with *Bus Type* dependant on *Bus Reg.*

ie. To put into third normal form the Log Table should be further split to put these fields into a table with information about each bus.

Together this gives

1. A **Route Table** with fields:

   Route -> Freq., Duration

   This table cannot be further normalised.

2. A **Bus Table** with fields:

   Bus Reg -> Bus Type

   This table cannot be further normalised.

3. A new **Log Table** with fields:

   Day+Time+Route+Direction -> Driver ID, Bus Reg

10.9 Restructuring The Log Table Into Boyce-Codd Normal Form

The Log Table has three possible keys:

either: *Day + Time + Route + Direction*
or: *Day + Time + Driver ID*
or: *Day + Time + Bus*

If the second key is chosen then *Route* is dependant on *Day+Driver ID* only, not on *Time.*

The Log Table should, therefore, be further split into:

1. A **Driver Allocation Table** with fields:

   Day + Driver ID -> Route, Bus

   This table cannot be further normalised.

2. A **Driver Log Table** with fields:

   Day + Time + Driver ID -> Direction

   This table cannot be further normalised.

This is not a very obvious division of tables!

Can the old Log Table be re-created to allow the driver or bus to be identified given a day, time, route and direction?

Yes - by joining the Driver Allocation Table and Driver Log Table by matching the *Driver ID* and *Day* fields .... a good use for a view!

10.10 Restructuring the Service Table Into First, Second and Third Normal Form

This table is already in first, second and third normal forms, with the key to this table being Bus Reg.

This has the same key and domain as the Bus Table derived from the original Log Table, so these tables should be merged to give a new Bus Table with fields:

Bus Reg -> Bus Type, Last Serv, Interval

But this table is not now in third normal form as *Interval* is dependant on *Bus Type*!

To put into third normal form these fields should be separated to give a table with the service table dependent on the bus type....

.... but this is the same key and domain as the Bus Type Table derived from the Permission Table, so these tables should then also be merged to give:

1. A new **Bus Table** with fields:

   Bus Reg -> Bus Type, Last Serv

   This table cannot be further normalised.

2. A new **Bus Type Table** with fields:

   Bus Type -> Capacity, Interval

   This table cannot be further normalised.

10.11 End Result After Normalisation

From the original four tables we now have:

1. **Bus Training Table** : *Driver ID + Bus Type*
2. **Salary Table** : *Grade -> Salary*
3. **Driver Table** :
   Driver ID -> Title, Name, D.O.B., Grade
4. **Bus Type Table** : *Bus Type -> Capacity, Interval*
5. **Route Training Table** : *Driver ID + Route*
6. **Bus Use Table** : *Bus Type + Route*
7. **Route Table** : *Route -> Freq., Duration*
8. **Driver Allocation Table** :
   Day + Driver ID -> Route, Bus Reg
9. **Driver Log Table** :
   Day + Time + Driver ID -> Direction
10. **Bus Table** : *Bus Reg -> Bus Type, Last Serv*

Although it has more tables this new structure will:

- take up less storage space,
- be easier to change and keep up to date,
- be less likely to contain errors!

CHAPTER 11

Introduction To 'SQL'

Contents Page

11.1 Introduction To 'SQL'

What is SQL?

- SQL is the Structured Query Language ....

  .... a very high level language to handle the data this language is known as a

  'Fourth Generation Language' or 4GL.

- It was originally developed by IBM for its DB2 database management system ....

  .... but later it became the ISO and ANSI standard language for database handling.

- There is more than one version of the SQL standard. This text describes the latest standard known as either SQL2 or SQL/92.

- This text does NOT describe every command and detail of the SQL/92 standard - this would be too complex for the space available, but it does describe all the commonly used commands.

- This text also describes some common additions to the SQL standard provided by widely used database management systems such as Access and Oracle.

11.2 Where is SQL Used?

- SQL the standard database query language used on most popular 'Database Management Systems' or DBS.

  Example of DBMSs using SQL are:

  Access, Oracle, Ingres, Unify, dBase IV, Paradox.

- A DBMS is a program or series of programs to create, modify and output data within a data base.

- A DBMS that handles databases in accordance with the rules for 'relational' data bases is called a 'Relational Data Base Management System' or RDBMS.

- A DBMS that supports the use of the 4GL such as SQL is known as a 'Fourth Generation Environment'.

- A DBMS that has facilities to build application programs, tailored to the users own needs, is known an 'Application Generator'.

11.3 What is a Database?

This term is not used in a consistent way.

It can refer to a single table . . .
(ie. equivalent to a single array of records)

. . . or it can refer to a collection of tables.

This text will use the following definitions:

A 'database' is a collection of data tables.

A 'table' is single array of records.

A 'row' is a single record in a table.

A 'column' is a field common in all rows.

A 'field' is a single column of a single row.

In some texts a table may be referred to as a 'relation', a record as a 'tuple' and a field as an 'attribute'.

ie. The following are equivalent:

Table	Relation	Array of records
Row	Tuple	Record
Column	Attribute	Field

11.4 Clients and Servers

Large database systems, such as Oracle, are frequently accessed as a "server" by other software known as the "client". This is particularly common on networked systems:

- The server holds all the data on a powerful central computer.
- The client gives the user interface application software communicating with the server from a smaller computer such as a PC.
- The client may have its own database facility used to keep local data accessible only to the user of that particular client computer.

A standard known as "Open Data Base Connection" (referred to as ODBC) gives a standard communication protocol between clients and servers.

Oracle conforms to this standard allowing it to be accessed by client software produced by many different software companies.

Examples of client software that can interface to Oracle or other ODBC servers are:

Visual Basic -	MicroSoft's software for generating Windows applications
Delphi -	Rival software from Borland
Paradox -	Another PC database package
SQL Windows -	Software by Gupta specifically written to be client software

11.5 SQL Language Syntax : Names

The data in a database is organised into tables and columns within the tables, each of which has a name.

On most SQL systems names of tables, column headings, etc. must:

- Start with a letter
- Contain only letters, digits and the underscore
- Be unique in 30 characters
- Be distinct from the many SQL reserved words

In Access/Visual Basic SQL names can include spaces, but in these cases the name must be enclosed in [] whenever used in an SQL command.

Tables names by default will refer to the users own tables.

Tables of other users can be accessed using:

username.tablename

but access will only be possible if permission has been granted by the table owner.

The '.' notation can also be used to refer to columns if the same column name appears in more than one table:

tablename.columnname

11.6 SQL Language Syntax : Commands

Case is not significant except inside string constants.

Commands are normally terminated with a ';'.

In Visual Basic SQL the ';' terminator is not required.

Commands may be spread over more than one line.

11.7 SQL Language Syntax : Constants

Number constants in SQL commands are as written:

eg. 42 or 1.234

String constants in SQL commands are enclosed in ' ':

eg. 'All my own work'

N.B. ' ' are not the same as " ".

' ' are used for string constants

' ' may also be used for dates

" " may have special uses on different systems.

In Visual Basic SQL " " can often be used instead of ' '.

11.8 Example Tables

The following two tables are used in the examples given in this text. These are the tables normally supplied with Oracle systems in the Oracle user area with user name "SCOTT" and password "TIGER".

The EMP table, a typical company personnel table:

Empno	Ename	Job	Mgr	Hiredate	Sal	Comm	Deptno
7369	SMITH	CLERK	7902	17/12/80	800		20
7499	ALLEN	SALESMAN	7698	20/02/81	1600	300	30
7521	WARD	SALESMAN	7698	22/02/81	1250	500	30
7566	JONES	MANAGER	7839	02/04/81	2975		20
7654	MARTIN	SALESMAN	7698	28/09/81	1250	1400	30
7698	BLAKE	MANAGER	7839	01/05/81	2850		30
7782	CLARK	MANAGER	7839	09/06/81	2450		10
7788	SCOTT	ANALYST	7566	09/12/82	3000		20
7839	KING	PRESIDENT		17/11/81	5000		10
7844	TURNER	SALESMAN	7698	08/09/81	1500	0	30
7876	ADAMS	CLERK	7788	12/01/83	1100		20
7900	JAMES	CLERK	7698	03/12/81	950		30
7902	FORD	ANALYST	7566	03/12/81	3000		20
7934	MILLER	CLERK	7782	23/01/82	1300		10

The DEPT table with details of the departments:

Deptno	Dname	Loc
10	ACCOUNTING	NEW YORK
20	RESEARCH	DALLAS
30	SALES	CHICAGO
40	OPERATIONS	BOSTON

11.9 The TABLE Command

Although it is not in the SQL standard many systems, such Access, provide a TABLE command which simply displays the content of a table.

Eg. `TABLE emp;`

This will display the contents of the emp table with suitable column headers.

This command is not available in all versions of SQL. If not available the simple alternative is to use the equivalent SELECT command:

ie. `SELECT * FROM emp;`

CHAPTER 12

Selecting Data From the Database With SQL

Contents Page

12.1 The SQL Command : SELECT

The purpose of this command to retrieve and display records from data tables.

The simple `SELECT` command format is:

```
SELECT select-list FROM table-name;
```

The `select-list` specifies which columns from the table are displayed and can be any of:

- * to indicate all columns in the table
- column name or names separated with commas
- real or integer number constants
- character string constants enclosed in ' ', (not "")
- number expressions with columns, constants, variables or functions combined with + - */ ( )
- character columns, constants, variables or functions concatenated with &
- dates enclosed in ' '
  (or in # # in Access/Visual Basic SQL)
- group functions

12.2 Multiple Columns and Column Headers

If more than one column is to be displayed the column names are separated by commas in the `SELECT` command.

The output is in a table form with one space between each column and a the column name as a header.

Each header is underlined with ---- to the width of the column displayed.

Most systems will allow a single word alternative header to be specified if the select-list option is followed by a space (in Oracle) or the keyword `AS` (in Access/Visual Basic) and new column header.

The system may allow alternative headers to contain spaces if the header text is enclosed in " " (in Oracle) or [ ] (in Access/Visual Basic).

Standard SQL select list examples:

```
*

ENAME, SAL, JOB
```

Oracle select list example:

```
SAL Salary, SAL*1.1 "New Salary"
```

Access/Visual Basic select list example:

```
ENAME, SAL AS [Basic Salary], JOB
```

12.3 Example Output From A SELECT Command

The SQL Command:

```
SELECT * FROM emp;
```

Would display the following output:

```
EMPNO  ENAME      JOB       MGR    HIREDATE SAL    COMM   DEPTNO
------ ---------- --------- ------ -------- ------ ------ ------
  7369 SMITH      CLERK       7902 17/12/80    800            20
  7499 ALLEN      SALESMAN    7698 20/02/81   1600    300     30
  7521 WARD       SALESMAN    7698 22/02/81   1250    500     30
  7566 JONES      MANAGER     7839 02/04/81   2975            20
  7654 MARTIN     SALESMAN    7698 28/09/81   1250   1400     30
  7698 BLAKE      MANAGER     7839 01/05/81   2850            30
  7782 CLARK      MANAGER     7839 09/06/81   2450            10
  7788 SCOTT      ANALYST     7566 09/12/82   3000            20
  7839 KING       PRESIDENT        17/11/81   5000            10
  7844 TURNER     SALESMAN    7698 08/09/81   1500      0     30
  7876 ADAMS      CLERK       7788 12/01/83   1100            20
  7900 JAMES      CLERK       7698 03/12/81    950            30
  7902 FORD       ANALYST     7566 03/12/81   3000            20
  7934 MILLER     CLERK       7782 23/01/82   1300            10
```

14 records selected.

12.4 Further SELECT Examples

Command: `SELECT * FROM DEPT;`

Output:

```
DEPTNO DNAME           LOC
------ --------------- -------------
    10 ACCOUNTING      NEW YORK
    20 RESEARCH        DALLAS
    30 SALES           CHICAGO
    40 OPERATIONS      BOSTON
```

Command: `SELECT LOC,DNAME FROM DEPT;`

Output:

```
LOC           DNAME
------------- --------------
NEW YORK      ACCOUNTING
DALLAS        RESEARCH
CHICAGO       SALES
BOSTON        OPERATIONS
```

Command: `SELECT SAL,SAL*1.1 FROM EMP;`

Output:

```
SAL
------ ---------------
   800             880
  1600            1760
  1250            1375
  2975          3272.5
  1250            1375
  2850            3135
  2450            2695
  3000            3300
  5000            5500
  1500            1650
  1100            1210
   950            1045
  3000            3300
  1300            1430
```

12.5 A SELECT Example With New Column Headers

The following Oracle Command:

```
SELECT 'Mr.'||ENAME "Name",
       'has new income' "has new income",
        SAL*1.1 "New Salary"
     FROM EMP;
```

Would display the following output:

```
Name           has new income New Salary
-------------- -------------- ---------------
Mr.SMITH       has new income             880
Mr.ALLEN       has new income            1760
Mr.WARD        has new income            1375
Mr.JONES       has new income          3272.5
Mr.MARTIN      has new income            1375
Mr.BLAKE       has new income            3135
Mr.CLARK       has new income            2695
Mr.SCOTT       has new income            3300
Mr.KING        has new income            5500
Mr.TURNER      has new income            1650
Mr.ADAMS       has new income            1210
Mr.JAMES       has new income            1045
Mr.FORD        has new income            3300
Mr.MILLER      has new income            1430

14 records selected
```

(Note: The || is the string concatenation operator in Oracle SQL)

12.6 The SELECT...WHERE Command

The WHERE clause is used on the SELECT command to specify which records are to be displayed.

All records are displayed if there is no WHERE clause.

The format is:

```
SELECT <select-list>
    FROM <tablename>
    WHERE <condition>;
```

Where <condition> is one of:

```
expression1 =  expression2
expression1 <> expression2
expression1 >  expression2
expression1 <  expression2
expression1 >= expression2
expression1 <= expression2
expression [NOT] BETWEEN value1 AND value2
expression [NOT] IN (value1,value2...)
column  IS [NOT] NULL
char_expression [NOT] LIKE template
```

These conditions can be combined with AND and OR.

A template is a character string used in matching character expressions that may contain characters with special meanings as follows:

Oracle	Access	Meaning
_	?	Matches a single character
%	*	Matches any number of characters
	#	Matches any digit

12.7 SELECT...WHERE Examples

Command:
```
SELECT ENAME, JOB, SAL
    FROM EMP
    WHERE SAL>=2000;
```

Output:
```
ENAME      JOB          SAL
---------- --------- ------
JONES      MANAGER     2975
BLAKE      MANAGER     2850
CLARK      MANAGER     2450
SCOTT      ANALYST     3000
KING       PRESIDENT   5000
FORD       ANALYST     3000
```

Command:
```
SELECT EMPNO,ENAME,JOB,
       SAL+COMM INCOME
  FROM EMP
 WHERE COMM IS NOT NULL
   AND COMM>0
   AND EMPNO IN (7499,7502,7519,
                 7654,7663,7701);
```

Output:
```
EMPNO  ENAME      JOB       INCOME
------ ---------- --------- ------
  7499 ALLEN      SALESMAN    1900
  7654 MARTIN     SALESMAN    2650
```

Oracle Command:
```
SELECT ENAME,JOB FROM EMP
 WHERE ENAME LIKE 'A%'
    OR ENAME LIKE 'B%';
```

Output:
```
ENAME      JOB
---------- ---------
ALLEN      SALESMAN
BLAKE      MANAGER
ADAMS      CLERK
```

12.8 The SELECT...ORDER BY Clause

The order of the records can be determined by the ORDER BY clause specified in the form:

```
SELECT <select-list>
   FROM <tablename>
   WHERE <condition>
   ORDER BY <column(s)>;
```

Order is descending if DESC is added at the end of the clause in the form:

```
SELECT <select-list>
   FROM <tablename>
   WHERE <condition>
   ORDER BY <column(s)> DESC;
```

If no ORDER BY clause is given the records are output in the order they are stored.

If more than one column is specified in an ORDER BY clause the output is sorted as follows:

1. The whole output is sorted on the first column mentioned following the ORDER BY.
2. For equal values of the first mentioned column the second ORDER BY column is used.
3. Similarly, where the first and second columns are equal the third column is used, etc.

In Access, unlike the WHERE clause, the ORDER BY clause can also be used in a TABLE command.

Eg. `TABLE emp ORDER BY ename;`

12.9 SELECT ... ORDER BY Examples

Command:

```
SELECT DEPTNO,ENAME,JOB,SAL
  FROM EMP
 ORDER BY DEPTNO,SAL DESC;
```

Output:

```
DEPTNO ENAME      JOB         SAL
------ ---------- --------- ------
    10 KING       PRESIDENT   5000
    10 CLARK      MANAGER     2450
    10 MILLER     CLERK       1300
    20 SCOTT      ANALYST     3000
    20 FORD       ANALYST     3000
    20 JONES      MANAGER     2975
    20 ADAMS      CLERK       1100
    20 SMITH      CLERK        800
    30 BLAKE      MANAGER     2850
    30 ALLEN      SALESMAN    1600
    30 TURNER     SALESMAN    1500
    30 WARD       SALESMAN    1250
    30 MARTIN     SALESMAN    1250
    30 JAMES      CLERK        950
```

Command:

```
SELECT DEPTNO,ENAME,JOB,SAL
  FROM EMP
 WHERE COMM IS NULL
 AND   SAL >= 1000
 ORDER BY DEPTNO DESC,SAL DESC,ENAME;
```

Output:

```
DEPTNO ENAME      JOB         SAL
------ ---------- --------- ------
    30 BLAKE      MANAGER     2850
    20 FORD       ANALYST     3000
    20 SCOTT      ANALYST     3000
    20 JONES      MANAGER     2975
    20 ADAMS      CLERK       1100
    10 KING       PRESIDENT   5000
    10 CLARK      MANAGER     2450
    10 MILLER     CLERK       1300
```

12.10 The SELECT DISTINCT Command

The DISTINCT clause on the SELECT command removes duplicate records from the display output.

The format is:

```
SELECT DISTINCT select-list
  FROM table
...etc. ;
```

Example:

Command:

```
SELECT DISTINCT DEPTNO,JOB
     FROM EMP
    ORDER BY DEPTNO;
```

Output:

```
DEPTNO JOB
------ ---------
    10 CLERK
    10 MANAGER
    10 PRESIDENT
    20 ANALYST
    20 CLERK
    20 MANAGER
    30 CLERK
    30 MANAGER
    30 SALESMAN
```

12.11 The `SELECT TOP n` Command

Visual Basic/Access SQL also offers `SELECT TOP n`.

This command outputs only the first `n` records of the select.

It is particularly useful when the output is ordered.

Example:

Command:
```
SELECT TOP 5 DEPTNO,ENAME,JOB,SAL
  FROM EMP
 ORDER BY DEPTNO,SAL DESC;
```

Output:
```
DEPTNO ENAME      JOB        SAL
------ ---------- --------- ------
    10 KING       PRESIDENT   5000
    10 CLARK      MANAGER     2450
    10 MILLER     CLERK       1300
    20 SCOTT      ANALYST     3000
    20 FORD       ANALYST     3000
```

12.12 Group Functions and the GROUP BY Clause

SQL offers a means of looking at summary results of all or part of a table by using group functions in a SELECT command:

COUNT(column_expression)	No. of non-null values
SUM(column_expression)	Sum of values
AVG(column_expression)	Average value
MAX(column_expression)	Highest value
MIN(column_expression)	Lowest value

eg.
```
SELECT MAX(sal),AVG(comm) FROM emp;

SELECT COUNT(ENAME) FROM EMP
   WHERE JOB='SALESMAN';
```

The SELECT command with the GROUP BY clause can be used to give summary results for selected groups of rows.

eg.
```
SELECT deptno,SUM(sal) FROM emp
   GROUP BY deptno;
```

The group function can be modified with the DISTINCT keyword:

eg.
```
SELECT COUNT(DISTINCT JOB) FROM EMP;
```

This will count the number of different jobs.

12.13 Group Function Output

Grouping over the whole report:

```
SELECT COUNT(*) "Number",
       SUM(sal) "Total"
    FROM emp;
```

would give an output (using Oracle) in the form:

```
Number Total
------ ------
    14  29025
```

(1 row of output only)

Grouping over selected ranges of records:

```
SELECT deptno, SUM(sal) "Total"
    FROM emp
    GROUP BY deptno;
```

would give the following output in Oracle:

```
deptno Total
------ ------
    10   8750
    20  10875
    30   9400
```

(1 row for each department in the emp table)

Note that the GROUP BY clause implies an ORDER BY on the same column(s).

12.14 Restrictions on GROUP BY Selections

As the `GROUP BY` clause causes only the summary information to be output the selected information must make sense in a summary.

ie. Selections are restricted to:

1. Group functions.
2. Constants.
3. Columns or column expressions also specified in the `GROUP BY` clause.

A group can be any size from a single record to the whole table.

A selection grouping can be made on multiple columns.

ie. To group by `deptno,job` will create a new group for every unique combination of `dept` and `job`.

12.15 The HAVING Clause

It is not necessary to display all groups on any column, groups can be selectively displayed with the HAVING clause.

The HAVING clause is similar to the WHERE clause except that it applies to conditions on groups.

eg.
```
SELECT deptno,SUM(sal) "Total Sal"
    FROM emp
    WHERE deptno <> 10
    GROUP BY deptno
    HAVING  MIN(sal) > 9000;
```

The HAVING clause should only be used with, and straight after a GROUP BY clause.

It is possible to use a HAVING clause where a WHERE clause could have been used:

eg.
```
SELECT deptno,SUM(sal)
    FROM emp
    GROUP BY deptno
    HAVING deptno <> 10;
```

is equivalent to
```
SELECT deptno,SUM(sal)
    FROM emp
    WHERE deptno <> 10
    GROUP BY deptno;
```

A WHERE selection is more efficient than the HAVING equivalent, however, so a WHERE should always be used *unless the condition contains a group function.*

12.16 The SELECT INTO Command

In Visual Basic/Access SQL it is possible to direct the output of a `SELECT` statement to create a new table.

The format is:

```
SELECT field1,field2...fieldn
    INTO newtablename
    FROM ..... etc.
```

The column names and types for the new table are the same as the data selected.

Note that if the table already exists it is completely overwritten by the new data.

Example:

```
SELECT ename,dname
    INTO NameAndDept
    FROM emp INNER JOIN dept
      ON emp.deptno=dept.deptno;
```

This will create a new table called `NameAndDept` with two columns, `ename` and `dname` with the same types as in the emp and dept tables.

Note: SQL/92 and Oracle also have an `INTO` clause when the SQL is embedded within a program. In this case it is a program variable rather than another table that is the destination for the data.

12.17 The `SELECT ... FOR UPDATE` Command

In Oracle, the `SELECT` command can be used to flag rows in a table that are to be modified by the user by adding an extra clause in the form:

```
SELECT ......
FOR UPDATE OF column1,column2,... [NOWAIT];
```

eg.
```
SELECT ename,sal,comm
    FROM emp
    FOR UPDATE OF sal,comm NOWAIT;
```

Notes:

- This command locks the rows so that other users cannot change the selected rows until the changes have been completed.
- The optional extra keyword `NOWAIT` prevents the system waiting while another user finishes their changes so that it can lock the selected rows.
- It is not essential to use this command before a modification is made to a table and for a single user system there would be no need to do so.
- This clause is not part of the SQL/92 standard and is not available in Access/Visual Basic.

12.18 The IN Table Qualifier

Visual Basic and Access normally store the data tables associated with a single database in a single file with a name xxx.MDB

In Visual Basic/Access SQL data tables in different files in the FROM and INTO clauses can be handled using an IN qualifier.

Examples:

```
SELECT * FROM emp IN C:\MYDIR\MYDB.MDB

SELECT ename,dname
    INTO NameAndDept IN C:\MYDIR\MYDB.MDB
    FROM emp,dept
    WHERE emp.deptno=dept.deptno;
```

Note: This is NOT part of the SQL/92 standard.

12.19 The Order of SELECT Clauses

The order of the clauses on a SELECT command is fixed and should always be as follows:

```
INTO   (IN)
FROM   (IN)
ON
WHERE
GROUP BY
HAVING
ORDER BY
FOR UPDATE OF
```

CHAPTER 13

Joining Database Tables Together

Contents Page

13.1 Types of Table Join

Oracle allows the `SELECT` command to display information from more than one table at a time.

The information from the two tables is said to be "joined" when more than one table is displayed.

There is more than one type of join.

The types are:

Inner Joins
- The Natural Join
- The Equi-Join
- The Theta Join

Outer Joins
- The Natural Left Join
- Other Left Joins
- The Natural Right Join
- Other Right Joins
- The Natural Full Join
- Other Full Joins

Cross Joins

13.2 The Natural Inner Join

This is the most commonly required join.

Two tables are joined such that all rows in each table are linked to the rows in the other table such that any columns with the same name have corresponding values.

Eg. If the `emp` and `dept` tables are joined with a natural join they would be linked where the common column, `deptno`, had the same value in each table.

The syntax in standard SQL for this would be:

```
SELECT * FROM emp NATURAL JOIN dept;
```

This would cause the columns from both tables to be matched with the common column listed once only.

Standard SQL also gives the option of specifying which columns are to be matched using the `USING` qualifier.

eg.
```
SELECT * FROM emp INNER JOIN dept
      USING deptno;
```

This would give an output similar to the natural join example as, in this case, there are no other matching columns anyway.

Unfortunately neither type of natural join syntax is available in Oracle or Access SQL!

13.3 Other Types of Inner Join

The other type of inner join available in standard SQL is where the join condition is explicitly specified.

The syntax is

```
<Table1> INNER JOIN <Table2> ON <condition>
```

Eg.
```
SELECT  * FROM emp INNER JOIN dept
    ON emp.deptno = dept.deptno;
```

This type of join is available in Visual Basic/Access SQL- but not in Oracle SQL.

If, like the natural join, the condition involves matching columns in the two tables as above, this is called the **equi-join**.

The difference between the equi-join and the natural join is:

1. The matching columns need not have the same name.

2. The matching columns from *both* tables will be listed, even though their values are identical if all columns are selected.

A join involving a comparison other than "=" is known as a **theta-join.**

13.4 INNER JOIN Example

Access/Visual Basic Command:

```
SELECT empno,ename,emp.deptno,dname
   FROM emp INNER JOIN dept
     ON emp.deptno=dept.deptno;
```

Output:

```
EMPNO  ENAME      EMP.DE DNAME
------ ---------- ------ --------------
  7369 SMITH          20 RESEARCH
  7499 ALLEN          30 SALES
  7521 WARD           30 SALES
  7566 JONES          20 RESEARCH
  7654 MARTIN         30 SALES
  7698 BLAKE          30 SALES
  7782 CLARK          10 ACCOUNTING
  7788 SCOTT          20 RESEARCH
  7839 KING           10 ACCOUNTING
  7844 TURNER         30 SALES
  7876 ADAMS          20 RESEARCH
  7900 JAMES          30 SALES
  7902 FORD           20 RESEARCH
  7934 MILLER         10 ACCOUNTING
```

(14 records selected.)

13.5 The Theta-Join

The theta-join is a join where a more complicated condition is used.

Eg. Suppose all managers are required to visit all the other departments.

An administrator may be asked to arrange the visits according to the following Access/Visual Basic command:

```
SELECT ENAME AS Name,
       'to visit' AS [to visit],
       LOC AS Place
   FROM EMP INNER JOIN DEPT
     ON EMP.DEPTNO <> DEPT.DEPTNO
   WHERE JOB='MANAGER';
```

This would give the following output:

```
Name        to visit Place
----------- -------- --------------
JONES       to visit NEW YORK
JONES       to visit CHICAGO
JONES       to visit BOSTON
BLAKE       to visit NEW YORK
BLAKE       to visit DALLAS
BLAKE       to visit BOSTON
CLARK       to visit DALLAS
CLARK       to visit CHICAGO
CLARK       to visit BOSTON
```

9 records are selected with every manager visiting every location but their own.

13.6 The `CROSS JOIN`

Standard SQL allows a cross join to be specified:

ie. `<Table1> CROSS JOIN <Table2>`

or simply: `<Table1>, <Table2>`

eg. `SELECT * FROM emp CROSS JOIN dept;`

or `SELECT * FROM emp, dept;`

In this example:

- Each line of output will contain all columns from both tables. ie. 8+3 = 11 columns

- As there are no `WHERE` restrictions the number of rows displayed will be:

  no.of rows in 1st table * no.of rows in 2nd table

  ie. every combination of a row from `emp` will be put with every row from `dept`.

  This will give 14*4 = 56 rows of output!

This type of join is also known as the "Cartesian Product", but it has few practical uses!

**Note: The "," syntax is an older form of syntax and is the only form of `CROSS JOIN` syntax recognised by Visual Basic/Access SQL.
The "," is also recognised by Oracle SQL.**

13.7 Converting a CROSS JOIN to an INNER JOIN

Any cross join can be made into an ordinary inner join by specifying the join condition in a WHERE clause:

ie.
```
SELECT ename, dept.deptno,
       dname, loc
    FROM emp INNER JOIN dept
      ON emp.deptno = dept.deptno;
```

is equivalent to:

```
SELECT ename, dept.deptno,
       dname, loc
    FROM emp CROSS JOIN dept
    WHERE emp.deptno = dept.deptno;
```

or:

```
SELECT ename, dept.deptno,
       dname, loc
    FROM emp, dept
    WHERE emp.deptno = dept.deptno;
```

The last syntax was the only format allowed in the earlier SQL standard (SQL/89) ....

.... it is still in common use today ....

.... and it is still the only format available for inner joins in many SQL systems.

The "," cross join modified by WHERE conditions is the only form of join allowed in Oracle SQL.

13.8 Inner and Outer Joins

Inner Joins

The examples so far given for the equi-join and theta-join have been *inner* joins.

An inner join means that if any entry in either table does not have a corresponding entry in the other table it is not listed.

eg. In the equi-join of `emp` and `dept` on `deptno` the Boston department does not appear in the output as there is no matching entry in `emp`.

Outer Joins

Entries that have no match in the joined table are output with null entries for the other table's fields.

An outer join in standard SQL is specified as a
`LEFT JOIN`, `RIGHT JOIN` or `FULL JOIN`.

A `LEFT JOIN` ensures all entries of the left hand table are output regardless of whether there is a match for it or not.

Blank fields are entered from the other table if there is no match.

Similarly, a `RIGHT JOIN` outputs all rows from the right hand table, and a `FULL JOIN` outputs all entries from both tables.

13.9 Outer Join Syntax

In standard SQL the `LEFT JOIN`, `RIGHT JOIN` and `FULL JOIN` can be specified with `NATURAL` as a qualifier or with `USING` or `ON` clauses.

ie.
```
<Table1> NATURAL LEFT JOIN <Table2>
```

or
```
<Table1> LEFT JOIN <Table2>
        USING <column(s)>
```

or
```
<Table1> LEFT JOIN <Table2>
        ON <condition>
```

However, in Visual Basic/Access SQL:

- **The `LEFT JOIN` or `RIGHT JOIN` can only be used with the `ON` clause**
- **The `FULL JOIN` is not recognised at all.**

eg.
```
SELECT empno,ename,
       dept.deptno AS dept,
       dname,loc
  FROM emp RIGHT JOIN dept
    ON emp.deptno = dept.deptno;
```

This will cause the Boston department to be listed with blanks for the `empno` and `ename` columns.

Note: `deptno` is specified to be from the `dept` table to ensure it is output on any "extended" entries.

13.10 Outer Join Example

Command:
```
SELECT EMPNO,ENAME,
       DEPT.DEPTNO,
       DNAME,LOC
  FROM EMP RIGHT JOIN DEPT
    ON EMP.DEPTNO = DEPT.DEPTNO;
```

Output:

```
ENAME       DEPT.D DNAME          LOC
----------- ------ -------------- ----------
SMITH           20 RESEARCH       DALLAS
ALLEN           30 SALES          CHICAGO
WARD            30 SALES          CHICAGO
JONES           20 RESEARCH       DALLAS
MARTIN          30 SALES          CHICAGO
BLAKE           30 SALES          CHICAGO
CLARK           10 ACCOUNTING     NEW YORK
SCOTT           20 RESEARCH       DALLAS
KING            10 ACCOUNTING     NEW YORK
TURNER          30 SALES          CHICAGO
ADAMS           20 RESEARCH       DALLAS
JAMES           30 SALES          CHICAGO
FORD            20 RESEARCH       DALLAS
MILLER          10 ACCOUNTING     NEW YORK
                40 OPERATIONS     BOSTON
```

15 records selected

Note it is possible to also have a `WHERE` clause on an outer join for conditions other than the join condition:

```
SELECT EMPNO,ENAME,
       DEPT.DEPTNO,
       DNAME,LOC
  FROM EMP RIGHT JOIN DEPT
    ON EMP.DEPTNO = DEPT.DEPTNO
 WHERE DNAME NOT IN ('SALES','RESEARCH');
```

13.11 Outer Joins in Oracle SQL

The LEFT JOIN, RIGHT JOIN and FULL JOIN syntax is not recognised in Oracle SQL so the standard, SQL/92 method of declaring outer joins is not possible.

Oracle provides an alternative syntax for an outer join, a (+) is put on the WHERE join condition.

Eg. The Oracle command:

```
SELECT EMPNO,ENAME,DEPT.DEPTNO "DEPT",
       DNAME,LOCATION
  FROM EMP,DEPT
 WHERE EMP.DEPTNO(+) = DEPT.DEPTNO;
```

This extends the marked table, EMP, with imaginary blank entries that will then correspond to all unmatched entries in the joined table, DEPT.

.... ie. The above is equivalent to a RIGHT JOIN.

(Note DEPTNO is specified to be from the DEPT table to ensure it is output on any "extended" entries)

In the above example if the WHERE condition was specified as:

```
 WHERE EMP.DEPTNO = DEPT.DEPTNO(+);
```

.... this would have been equivalent to a LEFT JOIN.

A FULL JOIN is *not possible* in Oracle SQL.

13.12 Table Alias Names

Tables can be given alias names by which they can be referred in the `SELECT` command.

eg.
```
SELECT empno,ename,De.deptno,
       dname,loc
  FROM emp Em INNER JOIN dept De
    ON Em.deptno = De.deptno;
```

In Access/Visual Basic SQL the "`AS`" keyword can optionally be used to specify the table alias name as in `emp AS Em` , but this is not essential.

Alias names may be used for the following:

1. For convenience, if a table with a particularly long name is referred to several times.

2. When a table is joined to itself, to distinguish which columns come from each use of the table.

   eg. To list an employees name with the name of his manager a table of manager employee numbers and names is required ....

   .... but this is available in the same `EMP` table.

   In Access SQL this could be obtained by:

```
SELECT slave.ename AS Employee,
       boss.ename AS Manager
     FROM emp slave INNER JOIN emp boss
       ON slave.mgr = boss.empno;
```

13.13 Example of a Table Joined to Itself

Access Command:

```
SELECT slave.ename AS Employee,
       boss.ename AS Manager
  FROM emp slave INNER JOIN emp boss
    ON slave.mgr = boss.Empno;
```

Output:

```
Employee    Manager
----------  ----------
SMITH       FORD
ALLEN       BLAKE
WARD        BLAKE
JONES       KING
MARTIN      BLAKE
BLAKE       KING
CLARK       KING
SCOTT       JONES
TURNER      BLAKE
ADAM        SCOTT
JAMES       BLAKE
FORD        JONES
MILLER      CLARK
```

(13 records selected.)

Note that there is no entry for `KING` as he has no manager and the join is an *inner* join.

To list `KING` with a blank for the manager field a left outer join is required:

```
SELECT slave.ename AS Employee,
       boss.ename AS Manager
   FROM emp AS slave LEFT JOIN emp AS boss
     ON slave.mgr = boss.empno;
```

13.14 Example of a Three Table Join

Joins can be extended to include three or more tables by replacing the name of a table with a nested join of tables in brackets.

eg.
```
SELECT slave.ename AS Employee,
       boss.ename AS Manager,
       loc AS Location
  FROM (emp slave INNER JOIN emp boss
        ON slave.mgr = boss.empno)
        INNER JOIN dept
    ON slave.deptno = dept.deptno;
```

or
```
SELECT slave.ename AS Employee,
       boss.ename AS Manager,
       loc AS Location
  FROM dept INNER JOIN
           (emp slave INNER JOIN emp boss
            ON slave.mgr = boss.empno)
    ON slave.deptno = dept.deptno;
```

Giving:

```
Employee   Manager    Location
---------- ---------- -----------
SMITH      FORD       DALLAS
ALLEN      BLAKE      CHICAGO
WARD       BLAKE      CHICAGO
JONES      KING       DALLAS
MARTIN     BLAKE      CHICAGO
```

....etc

Note: Any type of join (`INNER JOIN`, `LEFT JOIN` or `RIGHT JOIN`) can be nested inside an `INNER JOIN`.

But: It is *not possible* to nest any type of join inside a `LEFT JOIN` or a `RIGHT JOIN`.

CHAPTER 14

The SQL Data Maintenance Commands

Contents Page

14.1 The SQL Command : `CREATE TABLE`

New tables are created with the `CREATE TABLE` command.

This command creates an empty table and defines its structure.

The general syntax is:

```
CREATE TABLE table-name (column-details);
```

Where the column-details are a list of column names with the column types.

eg.
```
CREATE TABLE PERSON (
            ID_NUM  INTEGER,
            TITLE   VARCHAR(4),
            NAME    CHAR(10),
            DOB     DATE,
            NOTES   MEMO
            );
```

Possible column types are:

`CHAR(n)`	Fixed length string of n characters will be padded with spaces (n <=255)
`VARCHAR(n)`	Variable length string of n characters (n <= 255)
`INTEGER`	32 bit integer in the range ± 2G
`SMALLINT`	16 bit integer in the range ± 32K
`REAL`	Single precision real number
`DOUBLE`	Double precision real number

14.2 Date and Time Types

Earlier SQL standards had no date or time types. The SQL/92 standard introduces the following:

`DATE`	Holds a date with a 4 digit year.
`TIME`	Holds a time in hours, minutes and seconds.
`TIMESTAMP`	Holds both a date and a time.

Note, however, it is not uncommon to find, as in both Oracle and Access, that `DATE` fields can also hold times and that the above types are identical.

14.3 Additional Field Types

Visual Basic and Access also offer the following additional field types that are commonly found in other SQL systems:

`MEMO`	Variable length character string of any length. Only one field of this type is normally possible in a table. This is known as type `LONG` in Oracle.
`BYTE`	An integer in the range -128 to +127.
`MONEY`	A real number with fixed, two digit decimal places.
`BOOLEAN`	Holds 'True' or 'False'

14.4 Creating a Table from a SELECT Command

Although not part of the SQL/92 standard, most database management systems allow a table to be created from a SELECT command.

This enables the copying of part or all of one table to a new table.

Examples are:

Oracle has a CREATE TABLE ... AS command with syntax:

```
CREATE TABLE table-name (column-names)
     AS select-command;
```

Access/Visual Basic has a SELECT INTO command with syntax:

```
SELECT field1,field2...fieldn
    INTO newtablename
    FROM .....
     etc.
```

The column names and types for the new table are the same as the data selected.

Note that if the table already exists, its format and data are completely overwritten.

14.5 The SQL Command : `ALTER TABLE ... ADD`

Once a table has been created it is possible to add an extra column to the table using the SQL command:

```
ALTER TABLE table-name ADD column-details;
```

The new columns are added to the existing columns in the table.

All rows that already exist in the table will have null values created for the new columns. . .

. . . these may then be altered using the `UPDATE` command if required.

The column details are in the same format as in the `CREATE TABLE` command.

Examples:

```
ALTER TABLE EMP ADD FIRST_NAME VARCHAR(10);

ALTER TABLE DEPT ADD RENT MONEY;
```

Note: Both the `CREATE TABLE` and the `ALTER TABLE` commands can be used to create or modify table constraints as well as columns ....

.... constraints are discussed later under database integrity issues.

14.6 The Oracle Command :

ALTER TABLE ... MODIFY

A non standard Oracle command allows changes to the format of existing columns of a table. This is possible even though there are existing rows of data.

The syntax is:

```
   ALTER TABLE table-name MODIFY
              (column-details);
```

Columns with existing entries cannot change type or be reduced in width - they can only be made wider.

ie. Only if all rows have null entries for a column can that column change type or be reduced in width.

The ( ) round the column-details are not necessary for single columns.

Examples:

```
ALTER TABLE EMP MODIFY ENAME CHAR(12);

ALTER TABLE DEPT MODIFY
           ( RENT NUMBER(5),
             OWNER CHAR(20) );
```

Note: In Oracle SQL it is not possible to alter a table to remove columns.

14.7 The SQL Command : ALTER TABLE ... DROP

The `ALTER TABLE` command can also remove a column and any data it contains from a table.

The syntax is:

```
ALTER TABLE table-name DROP column-name;
```

Example: `ALTER TABLE EMP DROP COMM;`

Note: Although it is part of the SQL/92 standard the `ALTER TABLE ... DROP` command is not available in Oracle SQL.

14.8 The SQL Command : DROP TABLE

A whole table is deleted using the SQL command: `DROP TABLE`

The syntax is:

```
DROP TABLE table-name;
```

Example: `DROP TABLE DEPT;`

14.9 The SQL Command : INSERT

Once a table has been created, new rows of data can be added to it with the INSERT command with syntax:

```
INSERT INTO table-name (columns)
       VALUES (value-list);
```

or

```
INSERT INTO table-name (columns)
       select-command;
```

- The (columns) are optional, if omitted all columns are assumed.
- If the columns are named then any unmentioned columns will be set to NULL.
- The first format is used to insert one record at a time into the table.
- The second format is used to copy data from one table to add it to another.

Examples:

```
INSERT INTO dept
       VALUES (50,'FOREIGN','LONDON');

INSERT INTO emp (empno,ename,hiredate)
       VALUES (1234,'SANTA','25-DEC-95');

INSERT INTO My_Table (Name,Sal,Department)
    SELECT ename,sal,dname
       FROM emp INNER JOIN dept
         ON emp.deptno = dept.deptno;
       WHERE job='CLERK';
```

14.10 The SQL Command : `DELETE`

This command is used to delete rows from a table.

The general syntax is:

```
DELETE FROM table-name
   WHERE conditions;
```

Rows are deleted that match the conditions.

Warning:

If there is no `WHERE` clause **all rows are deleted**, the table will still exist but it will be empty.

Examples:

```
DELETE FROM emp;

DELETE FROM emp WHERE ename = 'WARD';

DELETE FROM emp
   WHERE comm IS NOT NULL
   OR    ename LIKE 'A%';
```

14.11 The SQL Command : UPDATE

This command is used to alter one or more columns in one or more rows of a table.

The general syntax is:

```
UPDATE table-name
   SET column-assignments
   WHERE conditions;
```

The column-assignments are a list of assignments separated by commas where each is in the form:

```
        column-name = new-value

or      column-name = NULL
```

Warning:

If no `WHERE` clause is specified **all** rows are updated.

Examples:

```
UPDATE emp SET sal = sal*1.1;

UPDATE emp
   SET job = 'MANAGER',
       sal = 3000,
       comm = NULL,
       deptno = 40
 WHERE ename = 'FORD';
```

14.12 Making Data Maintenance Changes Permanent

Changes made to a data base with INSERT, DELETE or UPDATE are all stored temporarily . . .

. . . they do not permanently alter the data!

To become permanent the following SQL command must be given:

```
COMMIT;
```

It is also possible to abandon all changes made in one session since the last COMMIT with the command:

```
ROLLBACK;
```

Some commands perform an implicit COMMIT command making all previous changes permanent.

These commands are: CREATE, ALTER or DROP GRANT, REVOKE OR EXIT

N.B. The COMMIT and ROLLBACK commands do not exist in Visual Basic/Access SQL.

From a Visual Basic program each command is immediately committed automatically unless the BeginTrans database function is used ....

.... in which case the database functions CommitTrans and Rollback provide the functionality of the SQL COMMIT and ROLLBACK commands.

CHAPTER 15

SQL Subqueries

Contents Page

15.1 Using a SELECT Subquery

The SELECT command can appear as part of other commands.

An example is the INSERT command:

```
INSERT INTO mytable (IDnumber,name)
   SELECT empno,ename FROM emp
    WHERE job='CLERK';
```

The SELECT command can, in fact, appear in any command with a WHERE clause such as DELETE or even SELECT itself:

```
DELETE FROM emp
 WHERE deptno =
       (SELECT deptno FROM dept
         WHERE dname='ACCOUNTING');
```

This example will delete all records from the EMP table of employees working in the accounts department.

In an example of this type it is important that the select command retrieves just one value, or an error will occur. . .

. . . It would not make any sense to have more than one value in such a comparison anyway.

15.2 SELECT Commands With SELECT Subqueries

The WHERE clause on the SELECT command can also contain a SELECT subquery.

Eg. To find all employees with a salary greater than Scott use:

```
SELECT ename,sal FROM emp
 WHERE sal > (SELECT sal FROM emp
                WHERE ename = 'SCOTT');
```

It is possible for the subquery to have further subqueries nested to any depth.

Eg. To find all employees with a salary greater than the manager of the accounts department:

```
SELECT ename,sal FROM emp
 WHERE sal >
       (SELECT sal FROM emp
         WHERE job='MANAGER'
           AND deptno =
               (SELECT deptno FROM dept
                 WHERE dname='ACCOUNTING'));
```

Note that the subquery can select from either the same table or a different table to the main SELECT command.

15.3 Subqueries With ANY, SOME or ALL

It is possible to use subqueries that may give multiple values if ANY, SOME or ALL is used:

Example of a subquery used with ANY or SOME:

To list all employees earning as much in salary as a manager:

```
SELECT ename,sal FROM emp
 WHERE sal >= ANY
       (SELECT sal FROM emp
         WHERE job='MANAGER');
```

In this example the WHERE clause will be true if the subquery search finds any manager's salary less than or equal to the salary of the record currently being examined.

SOME is simply an alternative word for ANY and has the same meaning.

Example of subquery used with ALL:

To list the employees with the minimum salary:

```
SELECT ename,sal FROM emp
 WHERE sal <= ALL
       (SELECT sal FROM emp);
```

This WHERE condition is true only if the salary of the record currently being examined is less than or equal to every value selected in the subquery.

15.4 Subqueries With `IN` and `NOT IN`

An alternative form for a multi-valued subquery is to use the `IN` or `NOT IN` conditions:

Eg1. To list every department that employs a clerk:

```
SELECT dname FROM dept
 WHERE deptno IN
       (SELECT deptno FROM emp
         WHERE job='CLERK');
```

Note: `IN (subquery)`
is another way of writing `= ANY(subquery)`.

Eg2. To list every department that has no salesmen:

```
SELECT dname FROM dept
 WHERE deptno NOT IN
       (SELECT deptno FROM emp
         WHERE job='SALESMAN');
```

N.B. This would not have been achieved with:

```
SELECT dname FROM dept
 WHERE deptno IN
       (SELECT deptno FROM emp
         WHERE job!='SALESMAN');
```

. . . as the sales department would be selected as it has some employees that are not salesmen.

Note: `NOT IN (subquery)`
is another way of writing `!= ALL(subquery)`.

15.5 The WHERE EXISTS Subquery

It is sometimes more convenient or natural to use a WHERE EXISTS or WHERE NOT EXISTS subquery.

In the WHERE EXISTS subquery if any matching record is found the result is true, so the column specification in the subquery is irrelevant.

Similarly the result is false if any matching record for a WHERE NOT EXISTS subquery is found.

Eg. To list every department with employees recorded in the EMP table:

```
SELECT dname FROM dept
 WHERE EXISTS
       (SELECT * FROM emp
        WHERE emp.deptno=dept.deptno);
```

This could also have been achieved using:

```
SELECT dname FROM dept
 WHERE deptno IN
       (SELECT deptno FROM emp);
```

Similarly to list departments that have no recorded employees:

```
SELECT dname FROM dept
 WHERE EXISTS
       (SELECT * FROM emp
        WHERE emp.deptno=dept.deptno);
```

This also has a NOT IN equivalent.

15.6 Subqueries Needing a Table Alias Name

If a subquery selects from the same table as the main query it may be necessary to use a table alias name.

Eg. To list all employees who manage other employees:

```
SELECT ename FROM emp AS boss
 WHERE EXISTS
       (SELECT * FROM emp
         WHERE emp.mgr = boss.empno);
```

In this example if the alias "boss" was not used the subquery would look for all employees who were their own managers!

15.7 Different Ways of Making a Subquery

A selection using a subquery may be done in different ways.

Eg. The following are equivalent:

```
SELECT ename FROM emp boss
 WHERE EXISTS
       (SELECT * FROM emp
         WHERE emp.mgr=boss.empno);

SELECT ename FROM emp
 WHERE empno = ANY
       (SELECT mgr FROM emp);

SELECT ename FROM emp boss
 WHERE empno IN
       (SELECT mgr FROM emp);
```

. . . and frequently the same information can be obtained just as easily using a table join:

```
SELECT DISTINCT boss.ename
  FROM emp boss INNER JOIN emp slave
    ON slave.mgr = boss.empno;
```

On large tables the different methods may give significant differences in speed and efficiency.

This is a disadvantage of SQL as it is confusing . . . .

. .users are unlikely to know which is more efficient.

Usually a `WHERE EXISTS` or `WHERE NOT EXISTS` subquery is more efficient than other methods.

15.8 Combining Selections With the UNION Operator

It is sometimes necessary to select information where each column of output may come from more than one table.

Eg. Suppose a company's database had tables:

CUST with columns CNAME for a customer's name
and CADDR for the customer's address
and

SUPP with columns SNAME for a supplier's name
and SADDR for the supplier's address

To list all outside organisations that the company deals with would require a selection from each table . . .

. . . but because a supplier may also be a customer for a different product, listing both tables with two SELECTs would give some names twice.

To give the required selection the **UNION** operator is used to combine SELECT commands:

```
SELECT cname AS Name,
       caddress AS Address
  FROM cust
UNION
SELECT sname, saddress
  FROM supp;
```

15.9 Example Output From a UNION

The command:

```
SELECT ename,empno FROM emp
UNION
SELECT dname,deptno FROM dept;
```

Gives:

```
ENAME       EMPNO
---------- ------
ACCOUNTING     10
ADAMS        7876
ALLEN        7499
BLAKE        7698
CLARK        7782
FORD         7902
JAMES        7900
JONES        7566
MARTIN       7654
MILLER       7934
OPERATIONS     40
RESEARCH       20
SALES          30
SCOTT        7788
SMITH        7369
TURNER       7844
WARD         7521
```

The command:

```
SELECT ename,job,deptno FROM emp
 WHERE job = 'CLERK'
UNION
SELECT ename,job,deptno FROM emp
 WHERE deptno = 10;
```

Gives:

```
ENAME      JOB       DEPTNO
---------- --------- ------
ADAMS      CLERK         20
CLARK      MANAGER       10
JAMES      CLERK         30
KING       PRESIDENT     10
MILLER     CLERK         10
SMITH      CLERK         20
```

15.10 Distinct Row Output With a UNION

A UNION implies a SELECT DISTINCT on the resulting output, any rows of output that are duplicated are eliminated.

ie. A row will be output only once if it is generated from both the SELECT commands.

The output will list duplicates if UNION ALL is used.

eg.

```
SELECT ename,job,deptno FROM emp
 WHERE job = 'CLERK'
UNION ALL
SELECT ename,job,deptno FROM emp
 WHERE deptno = 10;
```

would cause the row

```
MILLER     CLERK          10
```

to be output twice.

15.11 Column Headings With a UNION

If two columns with different names are combined using the UNION operator, it is the name in the first SELECT that is used in the column header.

The header used is the only effect of changing the order in which the SELECT commands are specified...

.... there is no difference in the rows displayed.

Any change of header using AS must be specified on the first SELECT command or it will be ignored.

15.12 Ordering the Output With a UNION

The UNION output is *automatically* ordered on the first column displayed unless this is changed with an ORDER BY clause.

It is not possible to specify individual ORDER BY clauses for each SELECT with a UNION operator but...

. . . a single ORDER BY clause can be used if it is at the end of the whole command.

eg.
```
SELECT cname,caddress FROM cust
 WHERE caddress LIKE '*Loughborough*'
UNION
SELECT sname, saddress FROM supp
ORDER BY cname DESC;
```

Note that the ORDER BY clause must refer to the column or columns in the *first* SELECT command.

15.13 Restrictions On The Use Of a UNION

1. The same number of columns must be selected from each SELECT command.

2. Corresponding columns of each SELECT command must be of the same type, though it is not necessary for the columns to be the same length.

3. Columns of type MEMO cannot be included.

There is *no restriction* on the number of SELECT commands that may be combined with UNIONs.

15.14 The INTERSECT and EXCEPT Operators

Like the UNION operator, the INTERSECT and EXCEPT operators operate on selections from more than one table and have the same restrictions and ordering.

Eg. To list all organisations that are both a supplier and a customer use INTERSECT:

```
SELECT cname "Name", caddress "Address"
    FROM cust
INTERSECT
SELECT sname, saddress
    FROM supp;
```

Eg2. To list all suppliers that are not also customers use EXCEPT:

```
SELECT sname "Name", saddress "Address"
    FROM supp
EXCEPT
SELECT cname, caddress
    FROM cust;
```

With UNION and INTERSECT it does not matter which SELECT is before or after the operator other than the effect on the column header.

For the EXCEPT operator the order is significant:

eg.
```
SELECT cname "Name", caddress "Address"
    FROM cust
EXCEPT
SELECT sname, saddress
    FROM supp;
```

This will select all customers who are not suppliers.

15.15 Oracle and Access Implementations of the UNION, INTERSECT and EXCEPT Operators

- Both Oracle and Access/Visual Basic implement the Union operator as described.

- Oracle implements the INTERSECT operator but Access/Visual Basic does not.

- Oracle does not implement the EXCEPT operator but does implement a MINUS operator that is identical in operation.

- Access/Visual Basic does not implement the EXCEPT operator and does not have any equivalent.

- In Access/Visual Basic the UNION operator can also be used to combine the output of two TABLE commands or a TABLE command with a SELECT Command.

  Eg.
  ```
  SELECT cname AS [Name],
         caddress AS [Address]
    FROM cust
   WHERE caddress LIKE '*Loughborough*'
  UNION
  TABLE supp;
  ```

CHAPTER 16

Views

Contents Page

16.1 What is a View?

A view is a "virtual table".

ie. A user can examine the data it contains as though it was a real table.

In reality it is a "window" onto one or more underlying base tables selecting and arranging the information in its own presentation.

The display of the information in a view is generated at the time it is viewed ....

.... *not at the time the view is defined.*

Any change to any base table data automatically changes the corresponding information displayed in any associated view.

Many Database Management Systems, such as Oracle, have the capability of creating these views and it is a standard facility of SQL systems.

N.B.: A surprising omission of Access/Visual Basic SQL is that views are NOT implement. However, the Access "Querydef" (which has to be created using Access facilities other than Access SQL) has similar properties to a view.

16.2 How is a View Created Using SQL?

By using the `CREATE VIEW` command in the form:

```
CREATE VIEW view-name (column-names)
   AS select command;
```

The select command in a view is identical to the usual SQL `SELECT` command with any clause *except* the `ORDER BY` clause.

The list of column names in ( ) can give new names to the columns in the view ....

.... they can be omitted, if they are the same names as the base table columns are taken.

Example of use of a view:

```
CREATE VIEW earnings (name,income)
    AS SELECT ename,sal+NVL(comm,0)
         FROM emp,dept
        WHERE emp.deptno = dept.deptno;
```

(`NVL` is as Oracle function used here to assign a value of zero to all null fields in the `comm` column)

Example of a view with grouped data:

```
CREATE VIEW totals (deptno,sal,comm)
    AS SELECT deptno,SUM(sal),SUM(comm)
         FROM emp
        GROUP BY deptno;
```

16.3 Why Create a View?

(1) Security

A view can restrict a user's access to a subset of the data in a table ....

.... users may be given access to a view where there is no access to the base table(s).

Example 1: Restricted access to columns.

A library data base may be available to public examination to allow users to see:

1. Which books are available
2. Which books are out on loan

but not 3. Who the books are on loan to

Example 2: Restricted access to rows:

Members of a university department may have access to inspect the university's accounts ....

.... but this may be restricted through a view so that only the transactions of that department can be displayed.

16.4 Why Create a View?

(2) Convenient Access to Joined Tables

When there is a need for regularly displaying data from two different, joined tables a view can create a permanent, virtual, composite table.

Example

There may be a regular need for details of a company's employees along with the details of their department ....

.... if this information is stored in two different tables such as the example "emp" and "dept" tables they could be combined into one by using:

```
CREATE VIEW mix_data AS
     SELECT number,ename,job,dname,place
       FROM emp,dept
      WHERE emp.deptno = dept.deptno;
```

16.5 Why Create a View?

(3) Saving Complex Expressions

There may be a requirement to regularly display complex calculated column expression values.

A view gives a means of "storing" the results of these expressions for easy access without using any storage space ....

.... as the storage is really only an illusion.

Example

The total income of each employee in the "emp" table could be saved in the following view:

```
CREATE VIEW emp_inc AS
     SELECT *, sal+NVL(comm,0) FROM emp;
```

(NVL is as Oracle function used here to assign a value of zero to all null fields in the comm column)

16.6 Why Create a View?

(4) Allowing Different Table Formats

A view can have a different, more convenient, format from that of the base table.

Example 1: Different order of columns

A table may have a column for a persons initials and a column for the surname.
Different users may require output in:

1. "Telephone directory" format of: Dawson R.J.
2. The conventional name order of: R.J.Dawson

If suitable views are created these could both be output by `SELECT * FROM view-name;`

Example 2: Different column formats

In Oracle there is a view called `USER_VIEWS` gives an output usually longer than one line if all columns are selected....
.... it may be more convenient to create a new view that truncates all columns to, say, half their length so that they fit on one line.

This would allow a quick look at the table through the new view in a format that would be easy to read and would serve most purposes....
.... however, where some important details are required that have been cut by the truncation, the full details are still available by accessing the original `USER_VIEWS` table.

16.7 Why Create a View?

(5) "Tables" of Summary Information

A view is a convenient way of "storing" grouped data such as totals, averages etc. using group functions - without actually using storage space.

Many database management systems have application generation facilities that will build default forms to handle the data in a single table ....

.... the use of a view based on group data may enable a default form to be similarly built to handle data from group summary data from a table.

Example

A company accounting data base may need a view to show numbers of transactions, totals and balances for each department.

This virtual table would be produced by a command such as:

```
CREATE VIEW summaries
    (deptname,transactions,balance) AS
    SELECT deptname,COUNT(*),SUM(trans)
        FROM dept_accounts
        GROUP BY deptname;
```

16.8 Why Create a View?

(6) Logical Data Independence

A view can be used to make a selection of command procedures and forms independent of the data format.

This is often introduced by necessity if there is a change in base table format as it may:

1. Save retraining users
2. Reduce the need to change any program that accesses the data.

Example

The `EMP` table could at one time have stored only the total income for each employee ....

.... later changes in circumstances may have created the necessity to split the income into its salary and commission components.

For this change it is possible to overcome the need to change any existing command files by:

1. Naming the new format `EMP` table as something other than `EMP`.
2. Creating a view called `EMP` on this new table that recreates the old emp format.

16.9 Data Updates Through a View

It is possible to insert or update data though a view in some circumstances.

If this is done it is the *base tables* that are really altered.

Rows can be updated providing:

1. The view is made up from one base table only.
2. None of the columns are derived from an expression.
3. The query to create the view contained no group function, no `DISTINCT` clause or no `GROUP BY` clause.

New rows can be inserted if all of the above applies and also if all columns constrained to be not null are included in the view.

But note: Rows can never be deleted from a view.

16.10 Deleting a View

Views can be discarded when they are no longer needed using the SQL command `DROP VIEW`.

Eg. `DROP VIEW my_view;`

CHAPTER 17

Performance of Relational Database Management Systems

Contents Page

17.1 Why Are Relational Databases Slow?

Relational database management systems are relatively easy to use . . .

. . . but they can be very slow in their operation.

Why?

1. The input commands have to be interpreted every time an instruction is given.

2. Data is stored in no particular order, this means that searches and sorts are repeated every time a command requires it.

3. Table joins are re-created for every instruction using the join - even joins made through a view.

   This involves a search through one table for a match for every record in the other.

4. Often no advantage can be made of available memory to store temporary tables, etc. as the system always uses disk storage.

5. The software is general purpose, no advantage is taken of particular features of an application for optimisation:

   eg. A search may only ever produce one record in a particular application - but the search will continue to the end of the table regardless.

17.2 Improving Access Time By De-Normalisation

Normalisation of data produces an efficient storage structure .... but it may not produce the most efficient structure for speed of access to the data.

In particular:

Displaying data from two joined tables requires stepping through one table and, for each record to be displayed, searching for a match in the other table....

.... this is very slow if many records are displayed!

Depending on the proportion of times the table will be accessed in this way it may be worth de-normalising by merging the tables.

Merging tables can be done in two ways:

1. Adding fields that are not dependant on the key if the resulting table has only a limited number of records.

2. Repeating fields if there is a limited number of values in a multi-value dependency.

N.B. Remember! This is not just a trade off of speed verses storage ....

.... it will also make the data more prone to errors of inconsistency!

17.3 Example 1: De-Normalisation by Adding Fields that are Not Dependant on the Key

If some normalised data gave the following tables:

Worker Table: *WorkerID -> Title, Name, DoB, Grade*

Wages Table: *Grade -> Wage*

If there are only 100 workers, the extra storage required to add the *Wage* field to the Worker table is negligible.

This would give fields:

WorkerID -> Title, Name, DoB, Grade, Wage

This now allows faster access to a workers wage....

but ....

- If there were only half a dozen grades the wages for each grade would be stored many times over.

  ie. Each time a wage for a grade was altered it would need to be changed in the table many times.

  This is an obvious source of potential error!

17.4 Example 2: De-Normalisation by Repeating Fields

If some normalised data gave the following tables:

Worker Table: *WorkerID -> Title, Name, DoB, Grade*

Training Table: *WorkerID + Qualification*

If every worker will never have more than three qualifications, the Qualification field could be repeated in the Worker table to give:

WorkerID -> Title, Name, DoB, Grade, Qualification1, Qualification2, Qualification3

This will allow faster access to a workers qualifications....

but ....

- It will waste space with blank fields if some workers have less than three qualifications.
- It may be more awkward to handle.

  Eg. Any search for a particular qualification would require searching all three qualification fields.

Another obvious source of potential error!

17.5 Improving Access Time by Using Indexes

What is an Index?

An index is formed on one or more columns in a table.

It is a table of row identifiers in the order of the given columns (the exact format is DBMS dependant).

Why use an index?

Once an index is made it is much faster to:

1. Sort the table on the given column(s).
2. Search the table for a particular column value - particularly significant for joins.
3. Select records using conditional clauses such as field_value < constant_value.

ie. The use of an index can greatly speed up a display command, especially for tables joined on the given column(s).

But is there any overhead?

1. Extra storage is required for the index equivalent to an extra column in the table.
2. Extra disk access means an index will only improve the speed of a display if less than 25% (approx) of the records are selected for display.

17.6 How is an Index Used?

On many database management systems the user need take no special action to use an index ....

The D.B.M.S. will use an index automatically where appropriate.

However an index may not be used if:

1. The index column is used in an expression
2. The column is tested to be `NULL` or `NOT NULL`

Sometimes it is possible to re-format a conditional clause so that an index may be used where its use was previously prevented. . .

. . . or vice-versa if it is likely that more than 25% of the records will be selected.

For example, if the column '`number`' was indexed the index would normally be used in the expression:

```
WHERE number > 200/1.15
```

but it may not be in:

```
WHERE number*1.15 > 200
```

and the index would normally be used in:

```
WHERE number > 0
```

but it may not be in:

```
WHERE number IS NOT NULL
```

It is up to the designer of database applications to know the behaviour of the system used.

17.7 Maintaining Indexes

Whenever any insert, update or delete is done it is necessary to update all the indexes for that table ....

.... most D.B.M.S.s do this automatically.

ie. Once an index is created the user can usually forget about it ....

.... the D.B.M.S. will do all that is necessary to use and maintain it.

17.8 Implications of Index Maintenance

Keeping an index up to date takes some processing time, every time any alteration is made to the table.

ie. In order to decide whether to create an index the balance must be considered:

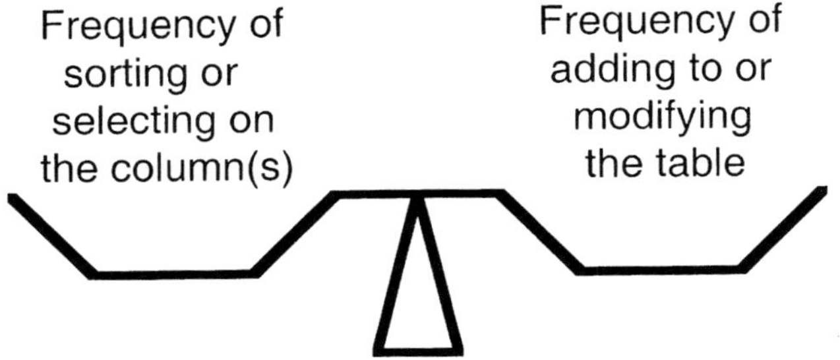

17.9 Different Types of Index

Unique Indexes

SQL allows an index to be specified as "unique".

A unique index is one where every entry in the column or combination of columns is unique ....

.... a unique index can be used more effectively for table searching, speeding up a search operation.

A unique index also helps preserve the integrity of a column by preventing any error of the same value appearing twice.

Additional Non Standard Index Types

1. Indexes in Oracle

   These can be "compressed", which takes less disk space, or "non compressed", which takes more space but allows faster searches.

   This can help to further improve performance.

2. Indexes in Visual Basic/Access

   These can prevent a column having null entries, can specify a column as a "primary" key or as a "foreign" key.

   This can help to secure the database integrity.

17.10 Creating an Index in SQL

An index is created with the SQL command:

```
CREATE [UNIQUE] INDEX index-name
       ON table-name  ( column(s) );
```

If more than one column is specified the rows are sorted in the order of the first mentioned column, then where values are the same, in the order of the second column, etc.

Examples:

```
CREATE INDEX nameidx ON emp(ename,deptno);

CREATE UNIQUE INDEX empindex
       ON emp(empno);
```

How Many Indexes Can a Table Have?

A table can have any number of indexes. . .

. . . but as each index takes storage space there may be limitations.

How is an Index Deleted?

The standard SQL command to delete an index is:

```
DROP INDEX index-name;
```

In Visual Basic/Access SQL, however, it is necessary to specify the table name in the `DROP` command:

```
DROP INDEX index-name ON table-name;
```

17.11 Improving Access Time by Optimising Queries

The structure and order of a query with multiple conditions as the selection criteria can effect the speed in which it can operate.

- A multiple selection criterion of the form:

  `WHERE condition1 AND condition2`

  will be faster if `condition1` eliminates more records than condition2.

- A multiple selection criterion of the form:

  `WHERE condition1 OR condition2`

  will be faster if `condition1` selects more records than condition2.

But .... if an index column is being tested:

- An indexed field should be tested before any other field.
- A unique indexed field should be tested before any non unique indexed field.

But note: *The D.B.M.S. may do this optimisation of indexed columns for you automatically!*

17.12 The Oracle Query Optimiser

Oracle will automatically try and optimise the order in which it tackles multiple queries as follows:

1. Indexed column queries come before non-indexed column queries.

2. Unique index queries come before non-unique index queries.

3. Non-compressed index queries come before compressed index queries.

4. `ROWID` queries come before column and expression queries.

5. Queries with = come before queries with a range of values.

6. Bounded range queries come before unbounded range queries.

Any ordering of queries by the user is only effective if the queries are "equal" by the above rules.

17.13 Optimising Join Queries

If there is a join of two or more tables then the join condition should be placed last.

Eg. Consider the workers example which had the following tables:

Wage Table: *Grade -> Wage*

Worker Table: *WorkerID -> Title, Name, DoB, Grade*

To find a worker's wage given his name the SQL command could be:

```
SELECT Name,Wage
  FROM Workers,Wages
 WHERE Workers.Grade = Wages.Grade
   AND Name = 'Bloggs J.';
```

This would join the entire `Workers` table with the `Wages` table and then, from the result, select the joined record for the name `'Bloggs J.'`.

Alternatively, it would be much faster to use:

```
SELECT Name,Wage
  FROM Workers,Wages
 WHERE Name = 'Bloggs J.'
   AND Workers.Grade = Wages.Grade;
```

This would select the single record from the `Wages` table with name `'Bloggs J.'` and then find the corresponding record in the `Wages` table.

17.14 Join Query 'Search' and 'Driving' Tables

When tables are joined in a query, either table can be the search table or driving table.

ie. The D.B.M.S. steps through every record in the driving table and looks for a match in the joined, search table.

The choice of which table is the driving table and which is the search table can greatly effect the speed of the query:

- If one of the tables is joined on an indexed column it is more efficient to make this the search table.
- If both tables are joined on indexed columns but only one index is unique, then this should be the column in the search table.
- If both columns are of equal type it is more efficient to make the table with the smaller number of relevant rows the driving table....

  ie. Reduce the number of searches to be made.

Often the order in which the tables are specified determines which is the driving table and which is the search table.

Example: 'Oracle' takes the first mentioned in the query as the search table.

But note: The D.B.M.S. may automatically optimise table joins involving an index.

17.15 Correct Use of the SQL SELECT Command

HAVING and WHERE clauses

In a query selecting group data the number of rows of output could be reduced by either a `WHERE` clause or a `HAVING` clause on the `SELECT` command.

eg.

```
SELECT deptno,SUM(sal)
   FROM emp
   GROUP BY deptno
   HAVING deptno > 10;
```

is equivalent to:

```
SELECT deptno,SUM(sal)
   FROM emp
   WHERE deptno > 10
   GROUP BY deptno;
```

But:

A `WHERE` selection reduces the size of the table by eliminating rows before the group data is calculated.

A `HAVING` clause eliminates groups only after all group data has been calculated....

.... throwing away some of the calculated data.

ie. A `WHERE` should always be used unless the condition contains a group function.

17.16 Improving Access Using Multiple Disks

If the database can be spread over several disks then access speed can be affected by the placing of tables and indexes on different disks.

Eg. Searching on an indexed column involves two disk accesses to obtain each record, one for the index and one for the table ....

.... faster access may be achieved by putting the index and table on different disks to minimise the movement of the disk heads.

For the same reason it may be effective to put tables that are frequently joined onto different disks.

17.17 Improving Access Time With a Single Disk

Some database management systems allow some control over tables storage on an individual disk.

Eg. Oracle achieves this by using of table "clusters" which store related data items that are used together in the same disk segment.

Clustering will usually improve access times, especially for tables joined on the cluster column....

and ... it may also reduce disk storage requirements

but ... you must know what you are doing or it can have the opposite effect!

17.18 Improving Access Time by Maximising Memory Use

Database management systems tend to be slow simply because disc space is the normal means for storing data.

Even if the hardware used has vast amounts of spare memory, this is usually ignored.

Some database management systems provide a means for using available memory, but the method is different for each system.

Eg. Oracle provides the `SET ARRAYSIZE` command to specifies how many records can be held in the host computer's memory at one time.

The default is 20 but up to 5000 can be specified.

Using the system's spare memory may be a simple way of improving performance if the D.B.M.S. provides this level of control.

CHAPTER 18

Designing the Database for Integrity

Contents Page

18.1 What is Database Integrity?

Database integrity is all about keeping the data meaningful and free from error.

Errors can come from two sources:

1. program error
2. human error

Program error can be eliminated by careful design and thorough testing ....

.... human error is harder to control!

It is possible for the database system to be designed to reduce the chances of human error:

- There may be checks built into the database management system that will automatically be used to reduce input error.
- There are further checks that can be added by the programmer when tailoring a database system to a particular users needs.
- The data structure design itself can reduce error.

This last method of reducing error can be achieved through *normalisation*.

18.2 Examples of Human Error Damaging System Integrity

Human error can damage the system integrity when:

1. The wrong input is entered.

   Eg. Entering a new employee with an ID number that is already used for another person

2. A modification is made that is incomplete

   Eg. Deleting a employee's record without altering other tables that refer to the employees ID number.

3. An inexperienced user changes the data without realising.

   Eg. A user may try to get out of the system by typing "exit" and accidentally insert the word into a database field.

4. More than one user at a time tries to alter the same data.

   Eg. Each may read the data at the same time to find the next free ID number and then each assigns the same number to a new entity.

All of these human errors can be reduced by careful system design.

18.3 Reducing Error With Default Values

One way of reducing human error is to minimise the need for manual input of data.

Eg. By entering a pre-defined default value in a table field if no value is otherwise specified in a new record.

In SQL/92 a default value can be specified when the column is defined in the `CREATE TABLE` or `ALTER TABLE ... ADD` commands.

If no default is specified then a null value default is assumed.

The format for specifying a column default is:

```
CREATE TABLE tablename (
    ............,
    columnname datatype DEFAULT value,
    ............);

ALTER TABLE tablename ADD
    columnname datatype DEFAULT value;
```

where the `value` is either a constant or `NULL`.

In Oracle SQL it is possible to modify the default value using the `ALTER TABLE ... MODIFY` command:

```
ALTER TABLE tablename MODIFY
    columnname DEFAULT value;
```

18.4 Default Field Value Example

The effect of the commands:

```
CREATE TABLE employee (
    empno INTEGER,
    ename CHAR(15),
    job   CHAR(10) DEFAULT 'CLERK',
    sal   INTEGER  DEFAULT 1000,
    dept  SMALLINT
    );

ALTER TABLE employee ADD
     comm  INTEGER DEFAULT 0;

INSERT INTO employee(empno,ename)
    VALUES (1234,'SMITH');

INSERT INTO employee(empno,ename,sal)
    VALUES (1235,'JONES',1200);
```

would be to create a new table with the following two rows of data:

empno	ename	job	sal	dept	comm
1234	SMITH	CLERK	1000	<NULL>	0
1234	JONES	CLERK	1200	<NULL>	0

N.B. The `DEFAULT` clause is NOT available in Access/Visual Basic SQL. However, an identical facility is available by setting the DefaultValue property for the table fields.

18.5 Reducing Error by Constraining the Data

The SQL/92 standard allows constraints to applied to table data.

The constraints are used to:

1. Check specified conditions relating to the table fields are always satisfied.

2. Check specified columns always contain unique values.

3. Specify table key fields and associated foreign key fields in other tables.

The constraints come in three forms.

1. Column constraints which refer to an individual column.

2. Base table constraints which refer to more than one field in a single table.

3. Assertion constraints which refer to fields from different tables.

Note: (1) is just a special case of (2), which in turn is a special case of (3).

But... Neither Oracle or Access/Visual Basic implements constraints of type (3).

18.6 CHECK Constraints

A CHECK constraint is specified for a column in the form:

```
CREATE TABLE tablename (
    ................,
    columnname datatype CHECK condition,
    ................);
```

Eg.
```
CREATE TABLE person (
    idnum  SMALLINT CHECK idnum > 0,
    title  CHAR(4) CHECK title IN
                ('MR','MRS','MISS','MS'),
    name   CHAR(20)
    );
```

A CHECK constraint for the base table is specified in the form:

```
CREATE TABLE tablename (
    columnname datatype,
    ...etc........,
    CHECK condition,
    ...etc........,
    );
```

Eg.
```
CREATE TABLE person (
    idnum  SMALLINT,
    title  CHAR(4),
    name   CHAR(20),
    sal    INTEGER,
    comm   INTEGER,
    CHECK title IN
                ('MR','MRS','MISS','MS'),
    CHECK sal+comm < 3000
    );
```

18.7 Notes on CHECK Constraints

1. The constraint will prevent any row being inserted into the table or being modified such that the constraint condition is violated....

   .... the error message generated, if any, will depend on the system.

2. In the SQL/92 standard the condition can be any type of condition that can appear in a `WHERE` clause.

3. In some database management systems, such as Oracle, conditions can not involve fields from other rows in the same table or any fields from other tables....

   .... this rules out the use of any select subquery in the condition.

4. Access/Visual Basic SQL does not implement `CHECK` constraints, but the same effect can be achieved by setting the validation properties of a table record or field.

5. Unlike other types of constraint (described later) there is no significant difference between a column `CHECK` constraint and a base table `CHECK` constraint.

18.8 Constraint Names

Each constraint can be given a name if the CHECK keyword is preceded by:

```
CONSTRAINT constraintname.
```

Eg.
```
CREATE TABLE person (
    idnum  SMALLINT,
    title  CHAR(4)
           CONSTRAINT tcon CHECK title
             IN ('MR','MRS','MISS','MS'),
    name   CHAR(20),
    sal    INTEGER,
    comm   INTEGER,
    CONSTRAINT scon CHECK sal+comm < 3000
    );
```

Constraints can then be dropped and base table constraints added using the ALTER TABLE command with a DROP CONSTRAINT or ADD CONSTRAINT clause.

Eg.
```
ALTER TABLE person DROP CONSTRAINT scon;

ALTER TABLE person ADD CONSTRAINT scon2
      CHECK sal+comm < 4000;
```

In Oracle column constraints can be modified as in:

```
ALTER TABLE person MODIFY CONSTRAINT scon
        CHECK sal+comm < 4000;
```

In Oracle a constraint cannot be dropped, but it can be disabled if the CHECK condition is followed by the key word DISABLE.

18.9 Assertions

SQL/92 also offers the ability to create CHECK constraints that are not attached to any particular table.

This is done with the CREATE ASSERTION command which has the format:

```
CREATE ASSERTION assertionname
   CHECK condition;
```

As it is not in the context of any table the condition necessarily involves SELECT subqueries.

Eg.

```
CREATE ASSERTION balance
   CHECK (SELECT startbalance
            FROM accountstable
           WHERE accnum=12345678)
       + (SELECT SUM(transaction)
            FROM logtable
           WHERE accnum=12345678)
       = (SELECT endbalance
            FROM accountstable
           WHERE accnum=12345678);
```

The assertion can be dropped using the command:

```
DROP ASSERTION balance;
```

<u>But</u> .... few database management systems implement this SQL/92 facility, and neither Oracle nor Access/ Visual Basic recognises the assertion commands.

18.10 Reducing Error with Mandatory Fields

In many Database Management Systems it is possible to prevent a null value being entered into a particular field ...

... this is particularly useful for key fields.

In SQL this is done by adding the words `NOT NULL` after the field type in the `CREATE TABLE` command:

Eg.
```
CREATE TABLE Person(
        fname  CHAR(20) NOT NULL,
        sname  CHAR(20) NOT NULL,
        salary INTEGER,
        comm   INTEGER);
```

These constraints can also be given names as in:

```
CREATE TABLE Person(
       fname CHAR(20)
             CONSTRAINT fnotnull NOT NULL,
       sname CHAR(20)
             CONSTRAINT snotnull NOT NULL,
       sal   INTEGER,
       comm  INTEGER);
```

The `NOT NULL` constraint is in fact a short form of writing:

```
CHECK columnname IS NOT NULL
```

so it can be dropped or added as a base table constraint as like any other `CHECK` constraint.

18.11 Access/Visual Basic Mandatory Fields

Access/Visual Basic SQL does not implement the `CHECK` constraint and, therefore, does not implement the `NOT NULL` constraint....

But .... it is still possible to define mandatory fields using an additional index facility.

In Visual Basic/Access the table must first be created with the standard `CREATE TABLE` command.

An index can then formed on the column or columns concerned with the extra syntax:

```
CREATE INDEX PersIndx
       ON Person(fname,sname)
       WITH DISALLOW NULL;
```

This would prevent either the fname or the sname fields being made null when a row is inserted or modified.

The index can be either an ordinary index or a unique index as required.

It can also be useful to create and then delete an index with the "`DISALLOW NULL`" option as a means of checking for null fields in the table.

It is also possible to achieve the same effect as the "`NOT NULL`" clause in Access or Visual Basic by setting the 'Required' property on a table field.

18.12 Reducing Error by Enforcing Unique Values

SQL/92 offers a form of constraint that enforces all column entries to be unique within a table.

A single column can be made to be unique in each row by adding the keyword UNIQUE in the column definition:

Eg.
```
CREATE TABLE person (
    idnum INTEGER NOT NULL UNIQUE,
    name  CHAR(20),
    sal   INTEGER
    );
```

A combination of columns can be made to be unique in each row by adding the UNIQUE base table constraint.

```
CREATE TABLE person (
    fname CHAR(12) NOT NULL,
    sname CHAR(12) NOT NULL,
    sal   INTEGER,
    UNIQUE(fname,sname)
    );
```

In SQL/92 specifying UNIQUE on a column means at most one row can have a null value for this column.

Alternatively some database systems assume:

1. The UNIQUE constraint also implies NOT NULL.

or 2. The UNIQUE constraint is not permitted unless NOT NULL is also specified.

18.13 Adding and Deleting UNIQUE Constraints

Like all constraints the UNIQUE constraint can be named, and in Access/Visual Basic SQL this must be done as in:

```
CREATE TABLE person (
    fname CHAR(12) NOT NULL,
    sname CHAR(12) NOT NULL,
    sal   INTEGER,
    CONSTRAINT key UNIQUE(fname,sname)
    );
```

This then allows the constraints to be dropped or added with the ALTER TABLE command.

Eg.
```
ALTER TABLE person ADD
    CONSTRAINT key UNIQUE(fname,sname);

ALTER TABLE person DROP CONSTRAINT key;
```

Most database systems implement the UNIQUE constraint by creating a UNIQUE INDEX with the same name as given to the constraint.

The above commands are therefore identical to:

```
CREATE UNIQUE INDEX key
       ON person(fname,sname);

DROP INDEX key;
```

Both Oracle and Access/Visual Basic implement the UNIQUE constraint by creating a UNIQUE index.

The error message, if any, for any attempted UNIQUE constraint violation will depend on the system.

18.14 Temporary Use of the UNIQUE Constraint

As the UNIQUE constraint is usually implemented with a unique index it has the same overhead as a unique index ....

ie. Extra disk space is needed and there is some delay on maintenance operations.

It may be useful, therefore, to create the constraint or index temporarily as a test for uniqueness....

....if the constraint or the index cannot be created then the column or columns are not unique and an error is generated....

....the constraint or index can then be dropped once the test has been made.

As a matter of good practice....

.... if the database system does not provide a UNIQUE constraint or index facility, a search should always be made to ensure any new value for a unique field does not already exist.

CHAPTER 19

Referential Integrity

Contents | Page

19.1 Reducing Errors by Knowing the Foreign Keys

Whether a table structure is derived with entity relationship analysis or by normalisation a knowledge of the key fields can help secure data integrity.

As well as its own key a table may have a field or fields that correspond to the key to another table....

.... this is called a *foreign* key.

When a record from a table is deleted, or a key field is modified it is essential to know which other tables contain the key field(s) as a foreign key....

.... **ALL** tables containing the corresponding foreign key will also need to be modified!

If these foreign key fields are left unchanged the database will loose its integrity.

If a record is to be deleted action must be taken to either:

1. Set the corresponding foreign key fields to null or default values.
2. Delete the records containing the foreign key values.
3. Prompt the user to enter another foreign key value.

19.2 Action To Taken When a Record Is Deleted

The action to be taken when a key field is deleted will depend on the tables and situation concerned.

Consider a company employee details table. The key field, the person ID, may be a foreign key in:

1. a table of previous jobs in other companies
2. a table of who drives each company car

Suppose a person record is to be deleted (he or she has left the company).

The previous job table entries for the corresponding foreign key value will only be relevant to that person.

ie. The corresponding previous job records can also be deleted.

For the company car table, the car will to continue to exist, so the car record cannot be deleted!

If a car can exist without being allocated to a person (it becomes a pool car) the record in the car table can be set to null....

.... otherwise the car must be reallocated to another person.

19.3 Master-Detail Tables

For some entities, instances of that entity only exist because of an instance of another, different entity.

These are **detail** entities, each owing their existence to a **master** entity.

There are two types of master-detail relationships:

1. A detail entity table where each instance is associated with only one of the master entity.

   Eg. A previous job table where each record corresponds to just one person entity record.

   Instances of previous jobs are usually created when the associated person instance is created.

   Such detail table records are deleted when the corresponding master record is deleted.

2. A detail entity table where each instance may be associated with several instances of the master entity.

   Eg. A job title table where each title may be associated with several person entity records.

   A job title is created when a person instance is created only if the job title does not already exist.

   Such detail table records would be deleted when no corresponding master records remain.

19.4 Preventing a Deletion

Suppose the company's employee records also contained a table of who had worked on which projects in the last month.

This project table is of historical interest so the records would need to be kept ....

.... but the record would make no sense without the details in the original person record ....

.... so the person record cannot be deleted!

ie. The foreign keys in other tables may mean a record cannot be deleted!

19.5 Action To Taken When a Key Field Is Modified

If a records key field is modified rather than deleted then the actions taken on corresponding foreign keys can be similar to the actions for deletion.

There is also the additional option of modifying the foreign keys in step with the original record.

Eg. Suppose the company employee record contained the key field of a company car record (rather than vice-versa as in the last example) ....

.... and suppose also the car registration number was the company car key field.

If the car is replaced, the registration number would change - and in this case the person record would need to have the same update.

Note: Modifying a tables key fields is questionable ....

.... is it really correct to do so?

In the above example it may be better to delete the old car's record and insert the new car as this more accurately reflects the real world action.

To preserve integrity it may be better to prevent any modification to any key field in any table!

19.6 Enforcing Referential Integrity

SQL/92 provides constraint facilities to enforce referential integrity.

ie. It ensures that every foreign key relates to a valid entry in the table it references.

In SQL/92 it is possible to specify the primary key for a table and foreign keys referring to fields in other tables.

This is done when creating the table:

Eg.
```
CREATE TABLE person (
          idnum INTEGER PRIMARY KEY,
          name  VARCHAR(20),
          deptno INTEGER
             REFERENCES dept(deptno)
          );
```

It is not possible to delete a record in a table if there is any instance of a reference to it by a foreign key field in another table.

Eg. If any record in the `person` table above has a `deptno` with value `10`, then the corresponding `dept` table record with `deptno` value `10` cannot be deleted.

But note - any error message generated will depend on the database system .... in Access/Visual Basic SQL <u>NO error message is given</u>.

19.7 Further Referential Constraint Syntax

The specification of primary and foreign keys can also be a base table constraint.

Eg.
```
CREATE TABLE person (
    fname CHAR(20),
    sname CHAR(20),
    deptno INTEGER,
    PRIMARY KEY (sname,fname),
    FOREIGN KEY (deptno)
        REFERENCES dept(deptno)
    );
```

This is the only way of defining multiple field keys.

Like other constraints, referential constraints can be named and handled in the `ALTER TABLE` command.

Eg.
```
CREATE TABLE person (
    idnum INTEGER
          CONSTRAINT pkey PRIMARY KEY
    name  CHAR(20),
    deptno INTEGER,
    CONSTRAINT fkey
       FOREIGN KEY (deptno)
       REFERENCES dept(deptno)
  );

ALTER TABLE person DROP CONSTRAINT fkey;

ALTER TABLE person ADD
    CONSTRAINT newkey
       FOREIGN KEY(name)
       REFERENCES employee(ename);
```

Note in Access/Visual Basic SQL all constraints <u>must</u> be named.

19.8 Notes on Referential Constraints

1. There can only be one primary key for a table but there can as many foreign keys as required.

   There can be any number of foreign keys in different tables referencing the same column or columns in one table.

2. A `PRIMARY KEY` constraint automatically makes the designated fields both `UNIQUE` and `NOT NULL`.

3. Most database systems create a unique index on the fields of the primary key constraint.

   The primary key can then be dropped with the `DROP INDEX` command.

4. Before a foreign key can be created it is necessary to either:

   - Create a primary key constraint on the referenced column(s) in the referenced table.
   - Create a unique constraint or index on the referenced column(s) in the referenced table.

5. If the column(s) in the referenced table are not specified then the primary key of the referenced table is assumed.

   Eg.
   ```
   CONSTRAINT fkey
       FOREIGN KEY deptno
       REFERENCES dept
   ```

19.9 The ON DELETE Clause

The SQL/92 default is to prevent the deletion of any row in a table if it has a field with a value referenced by a foreign key in another table.

Alternative actions can be specified, however, by adding one of the following to the foreign key definition:

```
ON DELETE CASCADE
ON DELETE SET NULL
ON DELETE SET DEFAULT
```

Eg.

```
CREATE TABLE person (
    idnum INTEGER PRIMARY KEY,
    name  CHAR(20),
    deptno INTEGER
        REFERENCES dept(deptno)
        ON DELETE CASCADE
    );
```

CASCADE means that when the delete is attempted on the row in the dept table referenced by the deptno field in the person table....

1. the delete in the dept table is permitted.
2. all rows in the person table that reference the deleted dept table row will also be deleted.

SET NULL also permits the delete in the dept table but then sets the corresponding foreign key fields in the person table to NULL.

SET DEFAULT is similar to SET NULL except the foreign key fields are set to their default values.

19.10 The `ON UPDATE` Clause

The `ON UPDATE` clause is similar to the `ON DELETE` clause except that it refers to the action taken when a referenced field is modified rather than deleted.

The SQL/92 default action is to prevent the modification, but this can be altered if any of the following are specified in the definition of the foreign key:

```
ON UPDATE CASCADE
ON UPDATE SET NULL
ON UPDATE SET DEFAULT
```

`CASCADE` permits the update and causes the foreign keys to be updated in step with the referenced field.

`SET NULL` permits the update but then sets the corresponding foreign key fields to `NULL`.

`SET DEFAULT` is similar to `SET NULL` except the foreign key fields are set to their default value.

19.11 Oracle and Access/Visual Basic Limitations

- Oracle only implements the `ON DELETE CASCADE` option. The other `ON DELETE` options and the `ON UPDATE` options are not recognised.

- Access/Visual Basic SQL does not implement the `ON DELETE` or `ON UPDATE` options, but it is possible to achieve cascade deletes and updates by setting relation attributes.

CHAPTER 20

Designing the User Interface for Integrity

Contents Page

20.1 Reducing Human Error With Automatic Generation of Identifier Values

It is very common to represent entities in a table with a unique identification value.

It is usually better if these identifiers are numeric.

Why?

1. Numeric values usually take up less storage space, and they are often repeated as foreign keys in other tables.

2. Comparing numeric values is usually a faster operation than comparing character strings.

3. It is easier to automatically generate the next free number when inputting a new record.

If there is an automatic generation of a new identity number the scope for human error is eliminated.

In order to automatically generate identity numbers it is common to have an extra table in the system with a name such as "identifiers".

This table will only have one record, with a field for every identifier required showing either the last used or the next free identifier value.

20.2 Re-using Identity Numbers

Question.: When a record is deleted how can an automatic system re-use the spare identifier?

Answer: **It must not do so!**

Such re-use is an open invitation for mistakes to happen....

.. *identity numbers should remain unique for all time!*

Eg. Suppose bank were in the habit of re-using an account number after someone closed their account ....

.... then one day a cheque, written by an original account number owner, is lost in the post but turns up much later ....

.... the new account owner will not be too pleased!

An identity number field may be defined to have only a limited number of digits - so it is conceivable the system will run out of numbers ....

.... **but**, it is far better to redefine the field to hold more digits than risk the potential confusion of re-using identity numbers.

20.3 Automatic Generation of Master Identifiers in Detail Tables

The generation of input "form" screens of many database management systems is based round forms that correspond to underlying tables.

Repeated attributes of an entity are normally put into a separate "detail" table which contains the key to the "master" table as a foreign key.

Eg. An employee master table may have an associated detail table of past positions held.

Input of a new "master" entity will therefore require input via several screen "forms", one for the master and one for each detail table.

To reduce human error on input the system should:

1. *Automatically* present the user with the each detail screen in turn when the master screen input is finished.

2. *Automatically* fill in the foreign master key fields in each detail table.

3. Ideally, allow the user to swap backwards and forwards between the master and detail screens.

This will allow the detail screens to be treated as an extension of the master screen.

20.4 Eliminating the Need to Remember Identifiers

Users of many database systems can be seen using a pen and paper to write down values read from the screen that they will need to enter later.

Eg. A company's employee records contain the addresses of each person. One employee gives his name and reports a change of address.

The database system operator may have to:

1. Select a search option.
2. Search through the records to find the employee's ID number.
3. Write down the ID number.
4. Select a modify option.
5. Enter the ID number of the record to modify.
6. Change the address.

This use of pen and paper is error prone and a sure sign of a poorly designed database system.

The system should have been designed to either:

1. Allow the user to enter modify mode directly from the search mode to modify the found record.

2. Allow the employees name to be used as an alternative to entering the ID number to identify the record to modify.

*However it is done, **all** need for operators to remember data should be eliminated.*

20.5 Reducing Input Error By Informing the User of Input Types

This can be achieved in a number of ways:

1. Providing Context Sensitive Help

Help for the current input field can be made available on part of the screen, or in a separate small window,

either: *automatically*, when the field is entered

or: *on request*, with a special key combination or button.

This is particularly useful to inform the user of the input type, such as the format for date input.

2. Identifying Mandatory Input Fields

Most input forms have some fields that must be filled in for the form to make sense and other fields that may be left blank.

It is possible to prevent the user putting a blank field into the database by specifying the field as `NOT NULL`

But ... it is less confusing for the user if the form:

1. Clearly identifies mandatory fields eg. by the use of colour.
2. Prevents the user moving to another field until an entry has been made.

20.6 Reducing Input Error By Displaying Input Values

1. Defaults

Default input values save time and help to reduce input errors, particularly on large forms or forms that are going to be filled in many times over.

SQL/92 provides a default facility to ensure a suitable default value is always entered into the database if the field is unspecified.

But... it is also useful to display the default in the input field on the screen so that:

1. The user knows the value of the default
2. The user can choose whether to overwrite the default or not.

2. Input Verification Fields

It is common for a user to enter an identification number to select a record for modification or deletion ....

.... but numeric values are easily miss typed.

In all such cases the user should be given an immediate display of other associated information, such as a name, to allow the user to verify the input.

20.7 Reducing Input Error By Checking Input Values

1. Input Field Type Checking

The database field types will prevent a user entering a value of completely the wrong type, such as a letter in a number field.

The application builder may also allow more sophisticated checking ....

Eg. Only allowing the letters and digits in the right places when inputting a national insurance number.

It is more user friendly to notify the user of the error immediately on exit from the input field rather than when the whole form has been completed.

2. Input Field Range Checking

This facility only allows sensible values to be input into a field....

Eg. Restricting an employee age field to be in the range 16 to 65.

The SQL/92 `CHECK` constraint can allow such checks to be made when putting the data in the data table....

But.... It is more user friendly to notify the user of the error immediately on exit from the input field rather than when the whole form has been completed.

20.8 Reducing Input Error By Restricting Input To a Limited List of Values

A textual input field often has only a limited number of valid input values.

Eg. "Manager" or "Clerk" could be valid in a person's job grade field but not "Boss".

Valid input is usually restricted to:

either a constant list of values.

or a list of values from a data table.

The `CHECK` constraint could be used to give an error if the input does not match one of the valid values.

But .... a more user friendly facility is to provide a pop-up (or pull-down) menu to allow the user to select the required value from a list.

Such a pop-up menu could be:

either automatic, popping up on entering the field.

or optional, popping up when the user requests it by pressing a particular key or clicking a button.

Note: The menu facility need not be compulsory....

.... many expert typists prefer a system which allows them the option of typing in values by hand, as for them it is quicker and more accurate to do so.

20.9 Password Protection

Password protection facilities may be provided as part of a Database Management System.

This will enable an application to be built to:

(1) Restrict access to authorised users.

(2) Give different users different levels of access.

Restricting certain users or categories of users to "read only" access can prevent unintended corruption of data by inexperienced personnel.

CHAPTER 21

Multi-User Systems

Contents Page

21.1 Problems With Multi-User Systems 1: Inter-Related Changes

Changes made to a system often come in "packages" that only make sense taken all together.

For example, a transfer of money from one account to another will involve two database changes:

- subtracting the money from one record
- adding it to the other.

ie. Two separate SQL `UPDATE` statements.

Even if this is done automatically within a single procedure on the client computer it will still take a finite time....

.... there is still time for another user to access the data in the meantime.

This danger increases with more complicated transaction packages.

To avoid this problem SQL has a means of making all the changes appear to other users to happen altogether....

.... this is called *transaction processing.*

21.2 Packaging Changes Into Transactions With SQL

A package of changes to a database using SQL is considered to be part of a single "transaction"....

.... each transaction can consist of several inserts, updates and deletions.

The transaction starts with the first table change....

....it ends when the `COMMIT` command is issued, it is only then that the changes are made permanent and the actual data changes are made to the table.

Until then ....

1. The changes are only visible to the user making the changes, other users see the table in its original unaltered state.

2. The user can wipe out the changes for that transaction by issuing a `ROLLBACK` command.

This packaging into transactions preserves integrity by making related changes appear to happen together giving a consistent view of the data to other users.

Eg. The transfer of money from one account to another will make the two database changes appear to other users to happen instantly.

21.3 Problems With Multi-User Systems 2: Simultaneous Changes By Different Users

A user may often read a value from the database then use that value to later change the database.

Eg. Suppose a 4GL banking system worked as follows:

First: Data is read from the database and displayed in fields on the screen

Then: The user changes the screen values

Finally: The user finishes by clicking a "save" button to update the database values.

But two bank clerks, Alice and Bert, read the same bank account total in quick succession.

Alice adds £100 to her copy.... Bert subtracts £50 from his.

Alice updates the account .... no problem.

Bert updates the account .... and wipes out the £100!

(Alternatively - if Bert had updated first then his £50 withdrawal would have been lost.)

What is needed is for the record to be locked when it first read so that no other user can update or lock that record until the changes are complete.

Another example:

Suppose a database program automatically provides an ID number when a new record is inserted.

The next available ID number is stored in a special database table.

First: The program reads the next unused ID number from the database and uses this as the ID number in the new record inserted.

Then: It adds 1 to the next available ID number stored in the database.

But if Alice and Bert both insert new records at approximately the same time.

Alice reads the next available ID number from the database ..... and Bert does the same.

Alice adds one to the next available ID number .... and Bert does the same.

The next available number is now 2 more than before

.... but the new records inserted by Alice and Bert have the same ID!

Again a lock is needed from the time the next available ID number is read until it updated.

21.4 Database Locking Systems

Most database management systems provide for some form of multi-user access, often this access is through a network.

To allow more than one user to make changes it is necessary to have an automatic system of locking out other users when any change is being made.

Different locking facilities may be provided depending on the database management system used and what action the user is taking.

How much of the system is locked can be:

- All data tables in the database system.
- A single table.
- A group of records in a table.
- A single record in a table.
- A single field of a single record in a table.

How long a table is locked can be:

- Until the user finishes accessing the system.
- While the user is working on the table.
- While the user works on the individual record.
- Until the user gives a command to "commit" the changes.

The type of locking can be to:

- Allow others "read only" access to the data.
- Prevent any access by other users to the data.

21.5 Automatic Locking During an SQL Transaction

Whenever a change is made to a table using the SQL commands `INSERT`, `UPDATE` or `DELETE` the affected rows are *locked until the transaction is completed.*

The extent of the lock depends on the database system.

Eg. Oracle and Access/Visual Basic both use a page locking system ....

.... which typically locks about 20 rows in the table.

This lock means that

1. Other users can only read the locked records .... they cannot change them until the transaction is completed.

2. If other users do read the locked records they always get the pre-change, pre-lock values.

The lock is released when the user issues a `COMMIT` or `ROLLBACK` command (or other command with an implicit commit such as the `CREATE TABLE` command).

This helps preserve integrity by preventing two users from changing the same data at the same time.

21.6 Locking With the SELECT FOR UPDATE Command

The SQL automatic lock only starts when the first change is made to the database ....

.... it does not solve the problem when changes are based on values that are first read from the database.

Many database systems, such as Oracle, extend the SQL `SELECT` command to lock rows in a table by adding the extra `FOR UPDATE` clause in the form:

```
SELECT ......
       ......
FOR UPDATE OF column1,column2,... [NOWAIT];
```

eg.
```
SELECT ename,sal,comm
    FROM emp
    FOR UPDATE OF sal,comm NOWAIT;
```

This starts a transaction with a lock such that only the user can then update or delete the selected rows until the transaction is completed.

The optional extra keyword `NOWAIT` prevents the system waiting while another user finishes their changes if it is already locked.

There is obviously no need to use the `SELECT FOR UPDATE` command in a single user system.

21.7 Access/Visual Basic Transactions

Transactions in Access/Visual Basic are activated in a non standard way under program control with the Visual Basic command:

```
<database_variable>.BeginTrans
```

eg. `mydb.BeginTrans`

There is no `COMMIT` or `ROLLBACK` command in Visual Basic/Access SQL, instead the equivalent Visual Basic commands must be used:

ie. `<database_variable>.CommitTrans`
and `<database_variable>.Rollback`

eg.
```
mydb.CommitTrans
mydb.RollBack
```

If these commands are not used Visual Basic/Access SQL automatically commits after every command.

There is also no `SELECT FOR UPDATE` command in Visual Basic/Access SQL .... a record can be locked for the period between a `SELECT` and an `UPDATE` by:

1. Starting the transaction with the Visual Basic `BeginTrans` command.
2. Locking the record with a dummy update such as:
   ```
   UPDATE emp SET empno=empno
      WHERE ename = 'SMITH';
   ```
3. Selecting the record and performing the updates as required.

21.8 Whole Table Locks

For complex action involving a whole table, many database management systems such as Oracle, provide a non SQL/92 standard table lock which be applied with the `LOCK TABLE` command:

```
LOCK TABLE <tablename> IN EXCLUSIVE MODE;
```

Only one user can apply this lock to a table at one time. Other users can still read the data but they will see it in its pre-change state.

Other, weaker locking modes may also be available.

The lock is released when the user issues a `COMMIT` or `ROLLBACK` command (or other command with an implicit commit).

The `LOCK TABLE` command does not exist in Access/Visual Basic SQL.

Instead the following non standard methods are offered:

1. Whole or part tables or groups of tables may be locked using member functions of Dynaset and Table variables.

2. An entire database `.MDB` file can be locked using extra parameters to the `OpenDatabase` function.

21.9 Problems With Multi-User Systems 3: The Need for a "Snapshot" View

Sometimes it is necessary to collect data from several tables in order to prepare a detailed report or perform a complex calculation.

Eg. An auditor may wish to examine all of a company's financial data which may be spread across many tables ....

.... but updates by other users made between the auditor's examination of the different tables could completely upset the figures.

To solve this problem some databases provide the SQL command `SET TRANSACTION READ ONLY;` which

1. must be the first command in a transaction.
2. prevents any command except `SELECT` from being used in that transaction.
3. provides a snap shot of the whole system at the time of the command ....

   all selects for the remainder of the transaction will show data as it was when the `SET TRANSACTION READ ONLY` command was issued.

N.B. This command is not available in Access/Visual Basic SQL .... A whole database lock would need to be used instead.

21.10 Problems With Multi-User Systems 4: Security Against Unauthorised Access

Many database management systems provide a means of giving individuals usernames.

Each table is "owned" by its creator - other users cannot access it without permission from the owner

In SQL permission is given using the following:

```
GRANT access-list ON table-name
    TO user-list;
```

where the access-list is either ALL or any combination of:

```
ALTER       DELETE      INDEX       INSERT
SELECT      UPDATE      UPDATE(column-name)
```

and the user-list can be either PUBLIC to give access to all users, or a list of user names.

Eg.

```
GRANT ALL ON MY_TABLE TO PUBLIC;

GRANT SELECT,INDEX,UPDATE(SAL,COMM)
    ON EMP TO OPS$corjd,OPS$corpk;
```

N.B. It is not possible to grant another user access to use the DROP TABLE command.

The GRANT command can also be extended with:

```
WITH GRANT OPTION
```

The `WITH GRANT OPTION` clause allows the other users you have granted access to use the `GRANT` command to pass the permission on to a third party:

Eg.
```
GRANT SELECT,INDEX,UPDATE(SAL,COMM)
    ON EMP TO OPS$corjd,OPS$corpk
    WITH GRANT OPTION;
```

The SQL command to remove access privileges is:

```
REVOKE access-list FROM user-list;
```

Eg.
```
REVOKE SELECT,UPDATE(COMM)
    ON EMP FROM OPS$corjd;

REVOKE ALL ON MY TABLE FROM PUBLIC;
```

21.11 Database Systems Without Built-in Security

Some database systems (such as Visual Basic) do not support the `GRANT` and `REVOKE` commands.

These systems rely on the usernames and filename protection of the operating system for security against unauthorised access.

Permission for other users to access database files must be given using the operating system commands - Eg. "filer" on the PC.

CHAPTER 22

Database Application Development

Contents Page

22.1 The Failure of Software Development

Statistics from DTI quoted in Software Engineering Solutions seminar:

For large software systems (>50K lines of code):

- Only 1% finished on time.
- On average they are one year late.
- On average they cost twice the original estimate.

Half the worlds software staff are involved in maintenance work....

.... at least half of this effort is non productive.

Most new software:

- Fails to meet aspirations of the sponsors.
- Fails to be accepted by users.
- Does not survive its anticipated life.

Is there no better way?

22.2 An Alternative Approach for Database Application Development : Prototyping

What is prototyping?

Prototyping is the process of transforming an idea into a model for purposes of developing, testing and communicating that idea.

How does it work?

It gives a visual representation that can be examined, and a working model of the interface of an application that can be tried out.

A pure prototype:

- is **not** the first version of the end product.
- is a throw away model built purely to try out an idea.
- is often referred to as a *rapid prototype*.

Why is it done?

Prototyping provides an effective method for generating feedback about what is good and what is bad about an idea.

It is often the only really effective way of doing so.

22.3 The Benefits of Prototyping

Prototyping can help in the following areas:

- Testing the feasibility of a solution idea
- Further developing a solution idea
- Communicating that idea to others
- Market analysis
- Testing a users reaction to a system
- Ergonomic and productivity testing
- Dividing the work into segments for different developers and for phased development
- Trying out alternative solutions
- Writing user and training manuals

It is particularly useful for the trying out ideas for the user interface ....

...... a notoriously difficult area to predict accurately as what seems right in theory can be quite impractical in practice.

22.4 Prototyping With Database Management Systems

Most database applications are built using:

either: the database management system's own built in fourth generation application generator.

Eg. *Visual Basic for Applications* in Access, *SQL*Forms* in Oracle

or: an independent fourth generation application generator that can interface to a database.

Eg. *Visual Basic*, *Delphi, SQL Windows*

or: a Web browser front end that interfaces to a database through an intermediate program.

Eg. *Netscape* or *Internet Explorer* interfaced with a program written in Java or Pearl.

These allow a fast development of the user interface

.... this is important for database systems because:

1. The database system itself may provide a fast and convenient means of directly generating default screens for handling a database table.

   ie. The database helps produce the user interface

2. The interface gives important clues about the data structure.

   ie. The user interface helps design the database

22.5 Prototyping and Database Design

Enter details for the new employee :- DONE

Name:

Sex: Date of Birth: Start Date:

Job Details
Department:
Job Title:
Grade: Salary:

Degree Qualifications
Type: Subject:
Institution:

The above is a typical screen that may be developed as a prototype for testing by a future user of an application.

Obviously it could uncover issues of usability such as:

- How do I abandon input of a persons details?
- How do I obtain help on using the system?

but

it can also uncover issues that directly affect the database table design.

22.6 Example Issues that Affect the Database Design

1. The user could point out that there is more than one person with the same name.

   This identifies a need for a ID number as an additional attribute.

2. The user could ask for new ID numbers to be generated automatically.

   This indicates the need for a single row table just to hold the last used ID number to enable the ID numbers to be generated.

3. The user may ask whether the surname should be put in first and whether first names or initials are required.

   This could lead to further enquiries identifying a need for separate surname and first name table fields.

4. The user may ask what format the dates should be in, which may reveal the information that dates in both the 20th and 21st centuries are to be stored.

   This indicates the full 4 digit year must be stored in any date attribute fields to be year 2000 compliant.

5. The user could object to filling in a long job title or department name and ask to enter a shortcode instead.

   This identifies a need for separate Department and Job Title entity tables.

6. The user could ask for the salary screen field to be filled in automatically as it can be calculated from the grade and job title.

   This indicates that the salary should not be in the person table, but in a table with the job shortcode and the grade as a multiple field keys.

7. The user could complain there is no way of entering a person with more than one degree.

   This indicates a need for a separate Degree Qualification entity table.

8. The user may try to leave some fields blank.

   This may indicate that some attributes are optional and perhaps should be made into separate entities to avoid too many null database fields.

22.7 How Is Prototyping Done?

To be more specific, the question is really:

How can a prototype be developed which provides a meaningful simulation of the real thing, and yet is produced so cheaply, in terms of time and effort, that a worthwhile saving is made on the whole project?

With hardware it is relatively easy:

> Development costs are small compared with mass production.

With software it is much more difficult:

> Mass production is very cheap compared with the high costs of development.

What is a reasonable cost for a prototype?

This will depend on:

- How effective it is in generating useful feedback.
- How much, if any, is reusable in the end product.

The high cost of software maintenance could justify spending up to a third of the development cost on throw away software ....

.... but for a fourth generation database system the reusable interface means the cost is rarely so high.

22.8 Using a 4th Generation Development System - *Is This Really Prototyping?*

With a fourth generation development system the screen design and layout of any prototype can be later used for the final system ....

.... can this be called prototyping?

Strictly speaking the answer is "no".

- It is not a pure prototype as it will not be thrown away

but ....

- often it is not the first version either as it may contain some throwaway code, eg. to place sample values in the screen fields.

It does not matter whether the prototype is pure or some hybrid ....

.... the important principle is that an early interface model is produced that can generate user reaction and feedback.

With these fourth generation systems there is so little cost when producing a prototype there is really no excuse for not doing so!

22.9 Prototyping Costs for Database Applications

A prototype of a database application developed with a fourth generation front end will consist of:

(1) The interface screens

These have no cost as they are reused

plus....
- they are produced quickly
- they can generate useful feedback

(2) Some working code reusable in the end product

This has no cost as it is reused ....

but....
- it can take a long time to produce
- a prototype looses value if it is not produced quickly

ie. Reusable, working code should be kept to a minimum in a prototype

(3) Some code to show samples of how the system would work.

This has a cost as it is thrown away ....

but ....
- it can often be produced very quickly
- it can generate useful feedback

ie. Throw away sample code is worthwhile if produced quickly

22.10 Prototyping Methods

How can a prototype be produced quickly with minimum cost?

1. Produce only part of the system

   Is it possible to partition the program such that a prototype can be built for part of the system?

   A prototype will usually be very useful even if it has nothing but the interface ....

   .... this is the part of the program most likely to generate useful feedback.

   Most database management systems have quick and easy to use facilities for building the user interface based on the table structure.

2. Use a reduced database

   A program may be greatly reduced if an in-memory database set up by hand, is used instead of a vast disk based database.

   Three, two or even one database record can be sufficient to show how the system would work.

   It may be possible to dispense with parts of the database altogether, if simpler data relations will suffice for demonstration purposes.

3. Simplify the development process

ie. Sacrifice quality and reliability.

The prototype is a *throw away* product, it does not need to be robust.

Even if the interface screens are to be kept the underlying code is often thrown away.

A hacked together program may be sufficient for a demonstration or user test.

But . . . if several prototype versions are eventually required, modifications from one prototype to another may be difficult.

4. Simplify data handling and error checking

The prototype is merely to show the user what will happen when the right and the wrong input is used.

It need handle only one example of correct input, and one example for each input error action.

Eg. It could treat "1/2/1997" as valid and treat *any* other date as an invalid date entry.

5. Ignore user input detail

   The modes of operating a system can still be shown even if the user text input is disregarded.

   A search could always "locate" the record for John Smith regardless which name the user requested.

6. Use alternative software to generate output

   Much of the user's feel of a program comes from it's output ....
   .... so a sample of the output can generate useful feedback.

   For example:

   Output onto paper - Use any word processor, drawing package or any other convenient software to create sample reports.

   Output to the screen - Even if it cannot do a thing, a sample screen or two created by any convenient software can generate feedback.

7. Use a modified version of another program

   A modification of similar application in a different context, even on a different computer, may be sufficient to generate user feedback.

22.11 Advantages of Prototyping

1. It is an method of extracting from the customer the application requirements that affect the database design and system operation which is:
   - Effective and more reliable than other methods
   - Often quicker than other methods

2. It is an effective means of checking the database design and system operation, identifying:
   - Misunderstandings between the customer and developer
   - Errors in the customer's specification
   - Omissions
   - Difficult to use features

4. Alternatives can be tested and compared using different try-it-and-see prototypes.

5. The early 'tangible' nature of a prototype:
   - Gives greater developer satisfaction
   - Pleases managers who like to see "progress"
   - Impresses customers
   - Helps communicate the developer's ideas to the customers.

6. Customer participation in the design process:
   - Helps the customers decide what they want
   - Helps the developer to know what the customers actually need
   - Helps the developer to know any customer eccentricities
   - Increases customer loyalty to the end product

7. The prototype can serve as a specification for the full production system which:
   - Is easily communicated to a team of developers without ambiguity
   - Enables developers to identify sections for splitting up the work between team members
   - Allows technical authors to immediately start on the documentation of user and training manuals

22.12 Disadvantages of Prototyping

1. *The prototype takes too much time and effort.*

   But for fourth generation database systems ....

   1. the speed which prototypes can be produced
   2. the ability to re-use much of the prototype in the end product (especially the screens)

   mean that prototyping will nearly always be cost effective.

2. *The prototype is confused with the real thing.*

   This could mean either:

   (a) The limitations of the prototype are taken as a reflection of the final product.

   ie. An overall bad impression is given.

   (b) The customer is pleased with the prototype and wants to use it.

   The developer may then be under pressure to further develop the prototype ....

   .... but later developments are based on a design which was full of compromises and never intended for further work.

   ie. It becomes a bodge!

22.13 A Real Life Prototyping Experience

Scene: A prototype has been shown which the customer likes so much the customer wants to use it.

Developer: *No you can't!*

Customer: *It's mine - I paid for it.*

D: *You can't, I'm not ready.*

C: *I'm going to - I can see it does what I want.*

D: *It's not documented!*

C: *I'll learn!*

D: *I won't be able to develop it - it'll all change!*

C: *It works at it is doesn't it?*

D: *Yes, but only bits of it - it's not finished.*

C: *Oh - why not?*

D: *It's a prototype!*

C: *But I can do xxx, yyy, and zzz can't I?*

D: *Yes* (.... mistake!)

C: *OK then I'll use that.*

D: *OK you can use the prototype to get used to using the buttons and to find out about how the system is used within Windows ....*

*.... it may **all** change ....*

.... do not 'go live' until I have developed the full system, only run it as a duplicate system.

C: *OK* (.... a narrow escape!)

INDEX

A

B

C

G

H

I

J

K

L

M

N

O

P

Q

R

S

T

U

V

W

Y